HOW TO STUDY MUSIC

HOW TO STUDY MUSIC

BY

CHARLES H. FARNSWORTH

ASSOCIATE PROFESSOR OF MUSIC, TEACHERS COLLEGE
COLUMBIA UNIVERSITY, NEW YORK CITY

INTRODUCTION BY

PROFESSOR FRANK M. McMURRY

AUTHOR OF
"HOW TO STUDY AND TEACHING HOW TO STUDY"

New York

THE MACMILLAN COMPANY

1920

AUTHOR'S PREFACE

Music soothes the child in his cradle; attracts him to the window when the street piano passes; when the band goes by, holds him spellbound, or carries him along with its swing. Why is it then that this preëminent art of the child should lose for so many children its fascination? Its charm seems to fade in the drab light of the schoolroom. There is often little in common between a child's joy in music and its study; the one appeals to the heart or perhaps to the feet, the other to the head. And how little the head is worth to a healthy child! Yet the two approaches to music should lead to the same end — its enjoyment should lead to a better understanding, and its study to a better enjoyment.

To aid in such a realization is the purpose of this book. To show the true relationship between real music and its study the plan has been adopted of describing the problems of music teaching by means of conversations carried on under the ordinary conditions of everyday life. The home is naturally a much more

appropriate place for illustrating such a treatment than the artificial limitations of the schoolroom. Both the conversational method and
the home surroundings are especially appropriate to an art, the study of which is rarely successful unless commenced in childhood, and one
that needs for its happy stimulation a sympathetic social life. The home is thus not only
the fitting cradle for the first expression of
music, but the most natural place for showing
the spirit in which it should be carried on.

It will be seen from the above that both the
conversational method and home surroundings
were chosen not merely to make a dry subject
attractive, but because such conditions made it
possible to explain the subject in a setting that
would make it more convincing. No attempt
is made to write a musical story with an educational moral; the conversations are merely
stagings for the thought. Often questions and
answers are introduced that from a story point
of view would seem very improbable, but they
are justified on the ground that a nearer repre-
sentation to life would have extended the narra-
tion without adding anything to the problem
presented.

When we consider the social and musical life
of the average American home, a feeling of
discouragement might arise for the future of

an art nurtured in such a cradle. But, fortunately, the home itself is coming to school. In the many subjects of everyday living that crowd the school hours, the seeds of more efficient homes are being planted, and it is hoped that the treatment of music appreciation, the picture of what the home may become through the wise study of music as suggested in this book, may help the teacher in applying those ideas that eventually will be the most important influences for better living, as well as finer music.

CONTENTS

CHAPTER I

The study of notation is often conducted in such a way as to produce a dislike of music and a misjudgment of its values.

The study of singing is often so conducted that it is thought of only as a clever thing to do, rather than as a beautiful expression.

Chorus practice in school is often so conducted that the opportunity is considered as a recreation period without standards.

Piano practice is often so done that it is thought of as drudgery without compensation.

There is frequently an attitude towards music that looks on it as a sensuous excitement, its value determined only by the individual's fancy, while musical production is looked on as an exhibition of skill.

Producing and listening to music as a family is a great help in making a united and happy home.

CHAPTER II

Music is an expressive art, hence when employed with poetry the latter must be understood.

Music is an art of the imagination, hence demands active coöperation on the part of the listener.

Music is an art of design, hence needs the development of the memory for grasping the design.

The most effective aid in order to grasp the form
of music is to memorize the motives from which music
is developed.

The most effective aid in order to grasp and retain
the content of music is to attempt to describe its
mood in some dramatic way.

Showing how meter is a practical device for deciding
the plan of the music and the relative duration of its
parts.

Showing how variation in duration is a part of the
design of the music and may be determined by aid of
the meter.

Showing how the feeling for key, or tonic, is essential
in deciding how the pitch varies and may be discovered
by anyone who goes at it right.

Showing how the pitch notation for the singer is a
device for measuring distance and not the names of
particular tones.

Showing how analyzing what is heard may help one
to enjoy music better by teaching one how to listen
and remember better.

Why singing to be of value must be beautiful.

The most essential thing to make the voice beautiful
both in singing and speaking is to have an intelligent
respect for what is to be uttered.

If the voice is injured it needs careful professional
guidance to free the student from bad habits of inter-

ference with what otherwise would be accomplished naturally.

The two forms of emphasis in teaching children to sing appeal to:

1. Knowledge; aiming at notation and sight singing.
2. Feeling; aiming at good song rendering.

Suggested compromise using a descriptive notation, thus developing thought without interfering with adequate imaginative expression in the early stages of the study.

CHAPTER V

   I. Preparation:
        1. Purpose to be accomplished.
        2. Use of one's own judgment.
        3. Proportioning the time to the work to be accomplished.
  II. Practice:
        4. Analysis: working on separate parts of the piece.
        5. Drill: making a study of difficult parts so as to do them without having to think about them.
        6. Synthesis: uniting the parts mastered so they will go well together.
        7. Application: testing one's work, for instance, by performance before others.

CHAPTER VI

   I. Active listening: doing something.
  II. Intelligent listening: knowing something.
        1. Information as to the purpose and origin of the composition.

INTRODUCTION

THE author of this book has been led to choose the title, "How to Study Music," rather than "How to Teach Music," because he is addressing the student rather than the teacher. His undertaking is difficult, on account of its newness; but he has been stimulated by the belief that it is only the student's method, after all, that really counts, and that future books on method must more and more represent this point of view.

Teaching is so intimately related to studying, that good teachers in any subject might be expected to understand quite fully how their pupils should study that subject. Indeed, with a majority of adults that statement is almost axiomatic.

There is, however, very little to justify such a conclusion. Skilled teachers, and even skilled trainers of teachers, have thought very little about how their pupils ought to study. Not one in a thousand would dare put on paper for publication the principal rules that should guide one in the study of any particular branch of knowledge. The attempt would be so crude that the author would be shamed. While method of teaching and method of studying are by nature very intimately related, they are far from identical; and an extensive knowledge of the one may be, and usually is, accompanied by a dense ignorance of the other.

Why is this true? There are numerous reasons; but one of the most important is that instruction has usually been considered only in terms of the teacher's activity. Lesson plans ordinarily have dealt only with the teacher's questions, suggestions, and directions; and books on method only with the teacher's method. In consequence, most teachers are hardly aware that children have a method, and very few of them can discuss instruction in terms of the learner's activity.

Yet the pupil's method of work is one of the principal things to which the educator should give attention; and his own method is of importance largely as it affects that of his pupil. It is at least a question whether books on method should not discuss mainly the learner's method rather than that of the teacher. Then the child would be held in mind as the real center of educational effort, rather than as something subordinate to the teacher and to the curriculum.

Then the young teacher would not need to struggle so hard in order to shift her attention from herself to her pupil.

F. M. McMurry.

Teachers College,
March 12, 1920.

HOW TO STUDY MUSIC

CHAPTER I

DIFFICULTIES IN THE STUDY OF MUSIC

Section 1

"I HATE music," emphatically cried Jack, as he entered the house, threw his schoolbooks on the couch, and started for the pantry. His mother, disturbed, and wondering what the trouble was, questioned him on his return.

"Why do you hate music?"

"It's a sissy kind of thing. The girls sing and the kids sing, but us boys don't unless we have to."

"You used to sing in the district school and I thought you liked it," said his mother.

"It was fun when you could shout, and all could pitch in together and make the tune hum; but here in the eighth grade, we are separated. Some of the biggest boys stay off on one side and sing bass, while I, with some of the smaller boys, sing alto-tenor, as they call it. Then the little kids and some of the girls sing soprano. When one part is singing one way and another

part is singing another way, it's all you can do
to keep together, let alone sing."

"But surely," said his mother, "after you have
learned the music it sounds finer than anything
you did in the district school."

"Well," he answered, "it may be finer, but
there is no snap to it, and the teacher keeps
telling us to sing up, and when we do, she tells
us we are singing wrong."

"I should think," said his mother, "if you
boys studied your music and learned to read,
you could sing right and have lots of fun."

"Perhaps the girls can learn how to read, but
we boys can't," Jack replied. "Mother, learning how to read music is silly stuff. You have
to do so many fool things, you don't know what
you are about. The teacher says, 'keep time,'
and then says, 'down, left, right, up,' and when
you get this to going, she wants you to sing at
the same time."

"Surely that is not hard," said his mother.

"But that's not all; she wants you to look
at the notes and say *do, mi, sol*. Sometimes
you go up when you sing them and sometimes
you go down and up. One time she will tell
you 'do' is on the line, and the next time that
'do' is on the space. And if you have learned
just how one note goes, you have to unlearn it
and learn something else. When we are singing

together one can make a bluff at it; but to-day the teacher asked me to sing alone and when I tried, all the boys laughed. I knew they were laughing, though they looked out not to let the teacher know it."

"Why should the boys laugh?"

"Because she asked me some questions about the time signature, and the key, and where 'do' was, and I had heard the same thing said in so many different ways that all I could do was to guess at it. I am willing to recite when I know a thing, but I don't want to be laughed at when it isn't my fault."

And Jack went out to forget his sorrows in baseball.

His mother remembered how he had sung when younger, and wondered whether his present dislike of music was not largely due to the method employed in teaching him. The family had moved into town early in the fall, for the special purpose of giving the children better school privileges, one of the most desired being a better opportunity for hearing and studying music.

The mother knew that it would be difficult for the children coming in from the ungraded schools to enter classes that would fit their needs. In all the subjects except music, however, careful attention had been paid to see that the necessary, prerequisite work had been done, while in music

Jack had been put in the eighth grade, knowing hardly anything about its technical side. Evidently there were no standards of requirement in this subject. As a result, the boy was being forced to attempt what he was not prepared to do.

As Mrs. Brown sat thinking this over, she was attracted by the humming of the little sister Nell, who was attending the first grade. She was sitting before a home blackboard, making curious marks and trying to carry a tune at the same time. To her mother's inquiry she replied,

"I am singing the Tulip Song and these are the tulips."

Her mother thought that there was some rhythmic connection between the syllables and the marks, but it was difficult to see the resemblance to tulips. Questioning brought out the fact that the teacher had used a little song for rhythmic purposes, making a dash with each pulse of the tune, in such a way that some of the marks looked like a row of tulips. This had interested the children; but, instead of drawing attention to the rhythmic character of the tune, and making that clear, the picture had drawn attention to itself so completely that its rhythmic illustration had been entirely forgotten.

"What else do you do in your music lesson?"

"We sing from the blackboard," said the little girl. "When the teacher writes 'one' we sing *do;* when she writes 'two' we sing *re;* and when she writes 'three' we sing *mi;* and we sing as far as eight that way. To-day she wrote the numbers on lines and spaces. I'll show you."

She drew a rough staff and put "one" on the first line and "two" on the space above it, and asked her mother to sing the appropriate names. In turn the mother took the pointer, and Nell played the part of the pupil, with great satisfaction.

"Mother, the teacher says I can sing these better than anybody else in the class. I just love to do it."

"But can you sing any song?"

"Yes."

"Suppose you sing me one."

She immediately started out on a trivial little tune with apparently no connection in her mind between the words and the expression of the melody. She breathed in the middle of words, and broke the phrases of the melody by singing as long as there was any air in the lungs, and then gasping for a new breath.

"Anybody can sing songs like that, but it's only the smart ones that can get *do, re, mi's* right," said Nell, with pride.

Her mother felt that her little daughter's music lacked the poetic aspects that make music valuable. She regretted that the child was not having the opportunity to learn those lovely songs that she had learned in childhood and enjoyed all her life. But there had been great progress in education; probably Nell was at the age when she should be taught technical matters, the lack of which was now embarrassing her brother. While such thoughts partially convinced her, there was still a misgiving that, perhaps now, this rather smart and matter-of-fact little daughter of hers might need, very much, to develop the poetic aspect of music.

"Can it be that this is not the most propitious time to awaken and cultivate the appreciation that she lacks?" she asked herself.

She was thinking of this, when her attention was drawn to her elder daughter, Harriet, practicing in the next room. Harriet was studying with a private teacher. Work under such conditions certainly must be more musical. She thought she would go in and see what progress was being made. She found her daughter, who had just finished her high school lessons, sitting in a listless and tired manner at the piano, with her little alarm clock before her, so that her eyes could rest upon it constantly.

"There, that finishes that," exclaimed the girl, with relief.

"Finishes what?" asked her mother.

"Oh, those horrid scales. I have to play them ten minutes before I do anything else. Now I have to put fifteen minutes on a study and then twenty minutes on my new piece before I can play over my old pieces."

Here, certainly, was system being carried out in a perfectly formal manner. The scales and study evidently had no connection in the pupil's mind with the difficulties to be overcome in the new piece. There was in each case simply a certain performance for so many minutes. She had calculated how many times the scales would have to be played to pass off a minute of time, and went up and down watching the clock and counting the numbers, the only aim being to make the best of a bad business.

"Mother, I don't see why I have to take piano lessons," was Harriet's rather discouraging complaint. "Most of the girls, when they get through their studies, go out and have a good time, but here I have to stay and do these stupid things, over and over. They don't help me a bit with my work in school. I have to do all that the others do and this besides. What's the use? I used to love to play before we came to town, but now I have to do these things, and think just how I must hold my fingers, and play so much that isn't interesting that I just hate it."

"But you like your school music, don't you?"

"Oh yes, we have lots of fun. It's almost like a recess. You know it isn't a regular study. We just attend, and we can do anything we want. When we like the piece, we all sing, at least all of us that can read. Lots of the boys won't sing and some of the girls would rather cut up than do anything else. It is so good to have one subject that you are not marked and examined in. It makes no difference whether you know it or not. The school is so large that we have divisions in music, and sometimes half of the class hasn't had note reading. While the teacher is showing those that don't know, those of us that do know, just have fun."

Poor mother! Alas, her dream of musical advantages for her children in town did not tally with what she was discovering.

Section 2

It was near Thanksgiving, and that evening Tom, the eldest boy, who was in college, was to come home on his vacation. He had

written with great enthusiasm that he was in
the Glee and Mandolin Club. His mother,
knowing how college education illumined history, science, and literature, imagined that
college music would bear a similar relation
to music in general. She knew of the boy's
work in the nineteenth-century poets; that
he was becoming familiar with some of the
gems of the greatest writers. He had told her
of his interest in Tennyson and Browning,
and she thought surely his college music would
arouse a love for the best examples of her be-
loved art.

She had never heard a Glee Club Concert.
The discrepancy between her idea of music
and what her younger children were accomplishing, made her longing especially strong
to get some satisfaction from what her big
son was doing. Realizing that only the talented boys of the college were in this musical
organization, she thought that when Tom
came home she would find that one member
of her family was getting real music and not
merely technique preparatory to its realization. That evening, therefore, it was with
considerable excitement that she watched her
handsome boy tune up his mandolin.

What she heard interested her, but it was
so different from what she had always thought

fine music to be! She was especially surprised at the curious names borne by the pieces that he played. The instrumental pieces were called "rags" with titles fresh from the variety shows, but, while they had a rhythmic go and dash that interested her, her hunger for music was not satisfied. Then he sang for her, and she laughed heartily at the humorous songs expressive of college life.

After that he passed on to sentimental songs with plenty of gush, but with no genuine poetry, or music. She noticed that his highest recommendation of a piece was that it was "the latest thing out." Even the high school sister had not heard of some of them. They were fresh from Broadway, with such ugly pictures on the title pages that she wanted to turn them over so she would not see them. She felt, somehow, that there was a relation between the vulgar prints and the words and poetry of the songs. She asked herself if this was college music. Surely this could not be the parallel of Tennyson and Browning. So she questioned her boy about music in college.

"Yes," he answered, "harmony is taught, but I don't know what it is. Only a few of the musical freaks take it. Then there is 'The History and Appreciation of Music,' a regular cinch of a course that everybody goes into that wants to make points. The professor tells them about music and gives them a few illustrations. But, Mother, there is far more fun in one rehearsal of the Glee Club than they get all year. Besides, my college adviser thought I had better not go into that course. He thought that since I had ability, — wasn't a regular stupid, you know, — I had better take a study that would tell. And he thought that I would get all the music that I cared for, and more too, in the Glee Club. He cautioned me not to spend too much time, but thought a little fun with the boys would be rather a help than a hindrance to my serious work."   .

Tom's father, who had been reading the newspaper, was pleased to think that his boy had so wise a counselor. He was not musical himself, but he did not object to a young man's having a little fun once in a while, and if the boy did not put in too much time, he did not see any objection to his being in the Glee Club.

Mrs. Brown thought over the musical situation of her family, and compared it with that of her own when she was a girl. She recalled how they all used to sing and play together. Her mother's ability with the piano; her father's fine voice; the skill of her brother, who played both piano and violoncello; and her sister's love of the violin, — what fun it was playing together!

Yet it was not the kind of fun that was appealing to her boy in his Glee Club. It seemed to her that a "Beethoven Trio" and a "Schubert Song" were something more than mere entertainments, just as are the poems of Browning or the lyrics of Tennyson. What had happened in this modern day, when so much improvement was supposed to have taken place, that her children's taste in music was so different from her own?

She could get little help from her husband, who seemed well satisfied with things as they were. But after she told him of the music she had had in her own home, early recollections came back to him of his old attitude toward music, which he had entirely lost in the stress of his professional career. So he readily consented to his wife's suggestion that they talk over the question of the family music with her musical brother, and see if things really were all right, and if it were she who was old-fashioned.

Thanksgiving day brought her brother to dinner, and she determined to present the problem of the musical experiences of her four children to him. His professional study of music made him able to judge the subject, while his freedom from the necessity to teach kept his relation to music always that of love and interest rather than that of one forced to regard the subject as a means of earning his daily bread. It kept him free from the hobby of method into which so many teachers, especially the conscientious ones, are likely to fall.

Mrs. Brown, who wanted music to follow the Thanksgiving dinner, suggested that they all sing together. While there were some tunes that the different members of the family knew, there seemed to be nothing besides the first stanza of "America" to which they all knew the words, and even of these not all were certain. This necessitated enough copies of the same book to go around, which proved difficult and took time.

By the time the page was found and the family ready to sing, the spontaneity and freshness of the whole act seemed to be lost. It was quite evident that some of the members of the family were taking part, not so much for their own enjoyment, as to please their mother. When it was suggested that they should have some solo work, Harriet, who was studying the piano, declared that she hadn't a single piece that she could play through. Moreover, the fact that their uncle was a proficient musician made the others shy about attempting individual work, as their mother at once realized. So, seeing that they wanted to start some Thanksgiving fun, she withdrew to an alcove with her brother, and rehearsed her musical perplexities.

Section 3

"Tell me, are my children going about it the right way in order to learn and truly enjoy music? Here's my boy Jack in the eighth grade, who says he hates music. He says that music study is only for girls and sissies, and is silly. On the other hand, Nell likes music, but is more interested in showing off her ability, in doing what we may call 'stunts,' than in singing. In fact, I do not think she has any idea what music is.

"Harriet, who is in high school, loves music and used to drum constantly on the piano; but since she has begun to take lessons in town and go on with her high school studies, she finds practice irksome, especially with a full program of school work. Her scales and studies are not done, so far as I can see, to help her play a definite piece, but for general technical proficiency. The result is that she plays by the clock, so many minutes of scales and so many of studies. Her high school music, on the other hand, seems rather to be an hour of recreation than an effort to gain musical skill or appreciation.

"But my greatest disappointment is that Tom, our college boy, who does so well in literature and history, has for music examples of the latest Broadway sensations, and while he is making and enjoying a certain kind of music, he knows nothing of such music as we valued in our old home. What completes this distressing situation is that Robert does not see why I care. I will not selfishly keep you away from the others, just now, talking on a subject that seems of little importance to them, but please think over my problem and advise me. Are you willing now to give us all a little music before the children go out to play?"

"Certainly," he said, and went at once to the piano. Remembering his sister's reference to Jack's estimate of music, he said he would sing a song by Schumann, called "The Two Grenadiers."

His reputation as a musician disarmed criticism and put everyone in a mood to accept what he gave them, however classical it might be. Even before the latter part of the song, where the stirring strains of "The Marseillaise" are introduced, everyone, including Jack, was thoroughly interested, and when this climax came, enthusiasm was unbounded. When the

song ceased everyone called for more. Then
followed a movement of a Beethoven Sonata,
a Chopin Mazurka, a Mendelssohn Song Without Words, and last, a lovely Schubert Im-
promptu.

The music that their uncle had been playing
was not the uninteresting stuff that all but
the mother had been expecting classical music
to be. They had been strangely moved. Here
was something different from the tinkling tunes
of the mandolin, and the songs written for the
children of the schools. There was a difference in the satisfaction each one felt. The
mother's delight made her speak of this difference in the pleasure produced by the different
kinds of music. The pleasure from popular
music was like that of eating a chocolate, or
drinking a soda, — a physical sensation.

But the pleasure from the music they had
just heard had in it much more than this. The
enjoyment of beautiful music made one forget
his petty individual self and become one with
the noble music he was hearing. It was an
enjoyment akin to that found in a glorious
mountain view attained after a hard climb.
There is a bracing, tonic effect in listening to
this kind of music, of which one is not conscious when hearing the light and popular
music of the day.

Harriet remarked that it took great talent to produce such music, and that ordinary people could not expect similar results. Her mother knew from her own experience, however, that this was not true. Such ennobling music had been a common experience to her. Hence she was anxious to have her brother explain the reason for the discrepancy between the musical experience of her own children and that of her childhood.

After the two children had gone out for their play, Harriet, Tom, and the older ones gathered around their uncle and talked about the music he had just been playing. At once, Mrs. Brown's thought went back to the question uppermost in her mind, and putting her query into words she asked:

"Do you remember what beautiful times we used to have with music when we were children; how it was the main, perhaps the most joyous feature of our family life? And while I am not complaining because my children are not musically talented, I am sorry not to have, in my own home, some of that pleasure in music that we had so much of when we were young."

Uncle Phil's memory of their youthful days came back to him; the delightful times of their early home life together. While his sister

c

had been telling how she felt the lack of such a common interest in her family, he had realized that it was not only appreciation that was lacking, but also much of the beautiful social life that music had been the means of focusing. The modern tendency to individualism was breaking up the family. Even the meals had become individual instead of social experiences. Each one ate by himself, when he was ready, so that it was difficult to keep the family together, even at the evening meal. Also the multiplication of societies — social, religious, philanthropic, and athletic — tended more and more to separate the members.

Mr. Curtis's first remark in reply to his sister's inquiry was to give her as much comfort as he could by saying:

"The difference between the present and the older home life is not peculiar to your family, Helen. There are influences at work tending to dissolve the family, and along with these influences are movements tending to give the individual greater freedom and opportunity. At the same time the necessity for careful thought for an adequate family life is more urgent now than ever; and I know of nothing so effective in cultivating this life as the ability to produce and listen to music together as a family group. Hence, the study of how to do this effectively, important as it is for our musical enjoyment, becomes doubly so when we think of its social bearing."

"What you say," said Mr. Brown, "interests me very much; for I see that, as the children are growing up, the family life which we enjoyed when they were young is disappearing. If music can contribute anything toward giving us a common interest and enjoyment, I am sure I should be most heartily in favor of it."

Mrs. Brown's face lighted up with an idea, and turning towards her brother she exclaimed:

"Why do you not act as our musical godfather and help us to get better musical results?"

He smiled at the form of her proposition, and yet he was pleased with the opportunity for such a practical demonstration of his own theories on music teaching.

"First," he said, "let me state the problems as they appear to me now, and we can see whether after consideration you would really like to take up the matter seriously."

Their hearty response showed that there would be no lack of support.

"The most subtle and pervasive influence in music, one that affects the taste and judgment of everybody, comes from the music we daily hear; so that the first and fundamental problem is: how to listen to music.

"Jack is almost swamped by the many difficulties in learning notation, which are making him dislike music; while Nell has a false enjoyment of music which is affecting what she likes and how she sings, and, what is perhaps the most serious result at her age, developing a bad instead of a good quality of voice. So, 'How to read notation' and 'How a child should sing songs' could be our second and third problems."

Then turning to Harriet, he continued:

"In order to get pleasure out of your piano study, 'How to learn to play the piano' should be the fourth problem; while the little respect that your high school music seems to call forth, shows that a fifth problem is involved in 'How to study in order to appreciate classical as well as modern music.'

"The fact that there is such a difference in the kinds of music that attract us, indicates that there is a difference in our musical experience that causes a difference in our tastes.

"It would help us to sympathize with each other, and keep us from getting narrow and biased in what we like in music, if we should consider this question. The problem might be put, 'How to select music so as to have respect not only for one's own feeling as to what is good, but also for the standards in the art, or what those who are best able to judge consider fine.'

" There is also one point more I want to make. That is, 'How to make use of music.' This is the most important suggestion that I shall offer, for in spite of the saying, 'art for art's sake,' I cannot conceive of music save as being a part of life itself. It is preëminently a social art. To produce it for sensuous or even artistic enjoyment in itself implies something selfish that prevents its having its most beautiful effect. Great art has always been wedded to great purpose of some sort. Music making in the home should above all be wedded to the social life of the home, not only for the benefit of the home life, but for the effect on the music, as well. Thus our last problem should give suggestions showing how all the preceding ones may be made more vital and effective. These problems presented in order, give such a list as this :

" 1. How to listen to music.

" 2. How to learn notation without awakening a dislike for music.

" 3. How a child should learn to sing.

" 4. How to learn to play the piano.

" 5. How to learn to enjoy classical as well as modern music.

" 6. How to select music.

" 7. How to make use of music in the family.

" If you are interested in considering these problems to see if you can get more satisfaction from music, both individually and as a family, I shall be glad to help you so far as I am able."

CHAPTER II

Section 1

A FEW days afterwards Uncle Phil came to commence the musical training of Nell and Jack. The children had been told that he was to explain how they should listen to music, and the novelty of the proposition appealed to them both. They were eager to know what he would say and do. The first thing Jack said after greeting his uncle was:

"I have seen cows and horses listen; they have to do something in order to hear; but I can't see why we should bother about it; we can't help hearing what is within hearing distance."

The picture of the cow listening so appealed to Nell that, as she was behind her uncle but still could see her brother, she commenced to go through lively antics representing the listening attitude of the pet cow they had in the country. This was rather disconcerting to Jack, who, however, was serious in his contention

23

that the subject they were to consider was hardly one that needed any attention from him.

"Very true," said his uncle, "we do hear all the sounds within hearing distance of our ears, for we can't shut our ears as we do our eyes so as to keep out the sounds we don't like. Let us see, however, if this is all there is in hearing. If I am not mistaken, on your way to school you pass the corner of South and Green Streets, where they have just commenced putting up a large block. You have certainly heard the foreign workmen talking to each other. It seemed more like the chattering of a lot of blackbirds than intelligent speech to you, and yet it was by means of this talk that these men were told what to do to lay the foundation for a fine building. Evidently while you heard all the sounds you did not really *hear* what was significant."

"Of course not," said Jack. "I don't know the foreign language that these men were using. But music isn't a language; you just hear it for the fun of it, and if you are near enough, you hear it all."

"That does seem so at first," was his uncle's reply. "Music does exist for the pleasure we get in hearing it. But there is a great difference in the enjoyment different people get from it. At a concert, for example, haven't you been bored by what you have heard, while some of the older people enjoyed it?"

Jack thought, and remembered a school concert where a long piano piece had been played that seemed so like a collection of unconnected stupid sounds that it was a relief to have it stop. Yet some in the audience seemed to think it very fine and clapped their hands for a long time after the player stopped. He had often been at church and heard people speak of liking the voluntary, or anthem, which to him seemed tedious beyond endurance.

"You see," said his uncle, "there is something more in listening to music than merely hearing the sounds. One must understand it, just as one must understand a language. It does not necessarily follow that we like what we understand. But if it is good music, we are likely to appreciate it. So it is quite possible that the trouble with the music you did not like was not the fault of the music, but because you did not happen to know that kind of musical language.

"There are, as you know, differences even in the kinds of English that one learns. What you hear in the streets in the rough parts of the city is very different from that which the minister uses in church; and haven't you noticed that some of your schoolmates are always using certain words incorrectly? In fact, haven't you been corrected when the proper way seemed difficult and wrong and you could not see why what you had been accustomed to was not just as good?

"In other words, the kind of English that a person likes and understands is the kind that he has been accustomed to. It is just the same with music. Some music is poor, being weak or sentimental; some is good, being strong or sensible. And those who have been accustomed to hear weak and sentimental music learn to like that kind. It seems all right to them, as incorrect forms of speech seem to others; while strong and sensible music, to those who are not accustomed to it, will seem stupid or senseless."

Jack, who often had to be corrected in the use of certain words, remarked with much satisfaction:

"Then it is your family's fault if you don't speak correctly."

"Partly," said his uncle, "but this is not all. Haven't you found that some of the poorer children in school, especially the brighter ones, while they come from homes similar to those of the others, learn to write and speak English much better than do the others? Why do you think this is so, when they come from the same kind of homes as the children that keep on speaking incorrectly?"

Jack reflected over this question and recalled to mind one of his chums, who, though he lived in the poor part of the city, where most of the people used incorrect English, still was far ahead of the other pupils in his ability both to speak and to write. He knew very well, from his knowledge of the boy, that this difference was not a matter of accident or luck, for the boy was one of those studious fellows who, when he set to work to learn anything, accomplished it.

His uncle continued:

"As one's English may be good because one comes from a refined and cultured home, so it may also be good because one has studied and paid attention to the way one speaks and writes. A person who enjoys good music may do so because he has come from a home where he is accustomed to hear good music, or he may enjoy good music because he has learned the difference between weak and sentimental, and strong and sensible music."

"Uncle Phil," asked Jack, "do you mean that by trying we can learn to like what we don't like?"

"Certainly, in the same way that you learn to use a correct form of speech. It requires attention, of course, and one naturally should not go on listening to weak and silly music if one wants to change one's liking for it. But especially, one should listen to strong and sensible music. It is wonderful how a little attention will make such music interesting. I will illustrate by singing something to you."

Then he sang Schubert's "The Erl King,"[1] using the English words. While the children could get the drift of the song, the rush of accompaniment and its dramatic character so excited them, that with all their interest there was also an element of confusion.

"That's great," cried Jack, filled with the spirit of the piece. "I don't see that we have to do anything special though, to listen to that."

"No," replied his uncle, "that music has words with it to tell you the story."

"Of course," said Jack, "somebody is riding, and carrying a child, — I don't quite catch the rest of it. It sounds as if some ghost was after the child, and the child died."

"That's practically the story," replied his uncle. "Now let me ask you some further questions and then I will sing the song again and see if you don't enjoy it more after you have

[1] "The Erl King" may be obtained through any large music store, published in collections of Schubert's Songs or as arranged for piano. It is also reproduced for the phonograph and piano player.

learned to listen. You have just said that you thought somebody was riding, — what in the music makes you feel so?" Their uncle played a little of the accompaniment to help them.

After some hesitation, Nell hummed the motion of the accompaniment to show that she felt that it represented the riding.

"Yes," said Jack, "that sounds as if the horse was cantering."

"How many characters are singing in the song?" asked Uncle Phil. "I'm singing all the words, but am I the same person all the time?"

The children, although they had felt the dramatic character of the song, had not thought how this had been brought about. The question of the singer's changing characters started them on a number of interesting observations.

"Sometimes," replied Nell, "you are the child, and then you are the father; and sometimes the one who tries to get the child."

"I am going to sing the song to you again in a moment. I want you not only to answer this question, — why the composer has given a different kind of music to each character, — but also to see if you can tell me how he has made the music fit the characters."

These questions brought about an attitude very different from the first. Both the little people paid better attention because it was focused on some definite problems growing out of the different characters presented by the poetry and illustrated by the music. Their uncle's aim was to get the children to listen to the music by the aid of poetic ideas. He went over the song again, the children listening for the different characters; how they were different and why they were different. This made them notice beauties in the accompanying music that they were only vaguely aware of when hearing the song the first time. Jack thought the father was carrying his son as if the boy were sick and frightened, "for when you take the child's character, you seem to call out as a frightened child would, while when the father sings, you sing as if you were soothing somebody; trying to quiet the child. And when the ghost" —

"That," said Uncle Phil, "is called the Erl King, the spirit.

"When he sings, the music is very beautiful and tempting, as if he were trying to coax the child."

"Isn't it wonderful," said his uncle, "that the music can make poetry seem so real and lifelike?"

The children were greatly delighted and wanted him to sing some more songs. But he

said, "I shall give you some others, soon, showing other things about listening. This illustration is only for my first point, that is, when
you are listening to anything that has words
with it, you must be sure to hear the words so
as to know what the music is about, and for
what you are to listen. This will make you
enjoy what you hear a great deal more. I am
sorry to say that in a great many concerts and
churches and Sunday schools, people listen to
the music just for the fun of it, and don't care
whether they hear the words or not. They
lose a great deal by that habit. If the song,
chorus, or anthem is a good one, you will find
that it pays many times over to know what
the words say that go with the music. This,
then, is the first thing to do in learning how to
listen. Whenever music and words go together,
be sure you find out all that the words can tell
you. If the words are in a foreign language,
such as we often hear in concerts, or in talking-
machine records, we may find out from the title
what the music is about and more from other
sources."

Section 2

"But music with words is only one kind,"
Uncle Phil went on. "Some of the most beautiful music does not have any words to help us

WILD RIDER
(WILDER REITER)

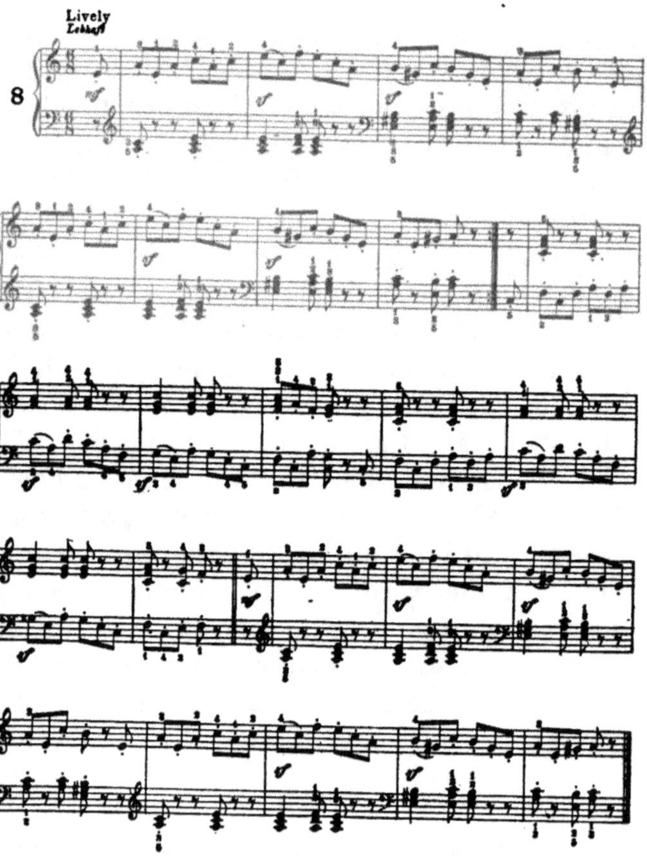

understand what it is about, so that we have to find out in a different way.

"I am going to play you a piece only a page long, by the composer, Robert Schumann, whose song you liked on Thanksgiving day. This is one of a group of pieces written especially for children, though grown people like them very much. Children like them because Schumann has given them something to do when listening to them. He has a name for each one of the little pieces, that tells you what the music is about, and it's great fun to see how the two go together. Instead of telling you the name of the piece and then playing it, I am going to play it first and have you think of a name that will go with it. We will see how nearly your name will resemble that of the composer."

Then he played "The Wild Rider." The children were a little mystified at the novel situation in which they found themselves. The piece sounded, as compared with what they were accustomed to hear, like an exercise or study; it was very short and almost seemed monotonous. Their uncle explained again what they were to do, — that they were to imagine that the piece was telling some sort of story, or acting out something, showing how something went, or how somebody felt. "Now," he said, "let me play it again."

D .

Nell responded with some enthusiasm, "It sounds like something going real fast."

"You are getting warm," replied Uncle Phil. "It is something going. What is it? A man, or a rabbit, or a horse, or a cow?"

Both children were on the track now. Jack suggested, "It can't be a cow, it might be a horse."

"Is he walking or cantering?"

The children were quite sure that he must be running.

Their uncle then said that Schumann called the piece, "The Wild Rider."

"Play another," said Nell; "this is almost as good as a guessing game."

"I will change the game a little," said her uncle. "I will write on this paper the names of two pieces. Then I'll play the two pieces and you can tell me which name goes with which piece. One is a boat song and the other a spring song. While they are called songs they are really little instrumental pieces written by a composer named Felix Mendelssohn."

He then proceeded to play "The Gondolier's Song" and the "Spring Song."

"That's easy enough," said Jack, "but I never listened to music that way before. It makes what you hear interesting."

"Yes," said his uncle, "let me play them again, and you see if you can pick out pictures on the wall that you would use if you were going to publish these songs and wished pictures for the title-pages, the way you sometimes see them on popular songs. You know something of the song from seeing the picture on the page, don't you?"

The children immediately commenced to examine everything pictorial about the room, while their uncle played the two pieces again. The photograph of a lovely Corot, with a figure dancing by the water in the early mist, was chosen by the little girl for the " Spring Song," and Jack liked a picture of a lone fisherman rocked by gentle waves on a wide expanse of sea, for the " Gondolier's." The boy remarked that he could hear the whistle from the fishing schooner that this boat belonged to, calling the fisherman back.

"But there's no schooner there," said Nell.

"No," said Jack, "but you can imagine. Don't you hear the whistle?"

"You can hear the whistle in the music, anyway," said his uncle.

"So in my picture you can see them dancing," said Nell, jumping about to illustrate.

"That was an easy one, though," said Uncle Phil, "for I had already told you that one was a spring song and the other a boat song. Still you see how music can give you something

to think of; not in the way grammar and
arithmetic do, but with fancy and imagination."

"Play something else and let us see if we
can tell what it is about without any help."

"All right, I will play you a piece by a Polish
composer named Frederick Chopin," and he
played a waltz having a little recurrent running
figure that whirled about fast enough to make
one feel almost dizzy. It glided off into a
second strain and then the first was repeated.
"Now can you give me a story for this?"

"That is certainly going some," said Jack.

"Yes," said Nell, "it seems to be going
round and round as fast as it can."

"What do you think the author called it?
'A little dog chasing his tail.'"

"Must have been a lively dog," said Jack.

"Yes," said Nell, "and I think he got tired
in the middle and then went at it again."

"Can you tell me of what value it is to listen
to music this way?" asked their uncle.

"It makes you pay attention to what you
are hearing, and it's fun too," answered Nell.
"It's like playing with dolls. You can make
believe and have all sorts of things happen."

"Yes," said Jack, his boyish nature asserting
itself in opposition to his sister's suggestion.
"But what is the use of all this make-believe?"

"It is very important in listening to music," replied his uncle. "Take the Sousa march that you heard on coming out of school. You don't care for it simply because it helps you keep step, do you? The use of music is not like that of a jackknife with which to make something. Its use is just the fun you get out of it. Now the fun you get in the march comes because everybody keeps step together, doesn't it? It is the 'skip and go' to the piece that you like to hear; everything happens just so, and you like it to happen that way, or you could not keep step to it. In this music that I have been playing, or a good deal of it, you don't want to get up and march to it, and it does not excite you, yet it pleases you, especially when you let the imagination or 'make-believe,' as your sister says, go with it. This kind of music needs that sort of make-believe to find all the pleasure that is in it. If you listen to it in the same way that you listen to the Sousa march, without any thought, and then feel your feet want to go, you will not get much from it. Most of the fine music needs your 'make-believe' with the sounds you hear. In these examples that I have been playing, we have been actually using names and stories and pictures, as a help. But if you practice listening to such music you will find by-and-by

that stories and pictures are not necessary and
that sometimes you cannot even state in words
the strange make-believes that come to you,
yet they seem so true and interesting that you
would not want to lose the fun of having them.
In fact, many people go to much expense and
trouble to hear music that affects them in that
way."

Section 3

"We have spoken of the importance of
understanding the words of a song, and also
of the value of 'make-believe' in listening to
instrumental music. But there is still more
to do. I don't mean by this that the imagination is not always at work, even with the kind
of music that I am going to play to you directly;
but what makes this new sort of music especially
interesting is that it calls upon us to use the
memory in a very active way. You will soon
see the reason for this.

"We have already spoken of music as being
like a language. The way music is put together resembles very much the way thoughts
are put together. There is, first, and most
important, the text. Some kinds of music
have a number of texts, and one text is spoken
about, or developed, for a while and then
another is taken up. These texts very often

contrast with each other, so we like to hear first one and then the other. But in the music that I want to play to you now, there is only one main text, or subject, and everything else must grow out of, or fit into it. It must be heard accurately the very first time it comes in, and remembered while the composer rings changes on it. This is no easy matter. It requires a lot of attention and a very good musical memory. Unless you notice and can remember the text, you won't enjoy the music as you should, though you might hear parts here and there that pleased you, in the way that you might catch the minister's illustrations here and there without knowing to what they were related.

"The main feature, then, about this music is, that you must notice the text and remember it. Now, I will play."

The children stood on either side of their uncle with astonishment on their faces, for they had never dreamed of such a thing in music. When the uncle had finished the piece, which lasted only about a minute, there was most decided disappointment on both faces. Jack declared that it was only a jumble of noises, and Nell said, "I don't see how you tried to do anything but to see how fast you could wiggle your fingers."

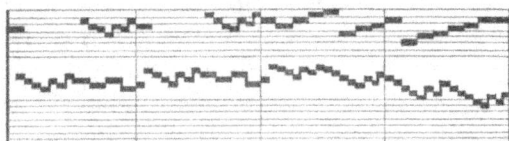

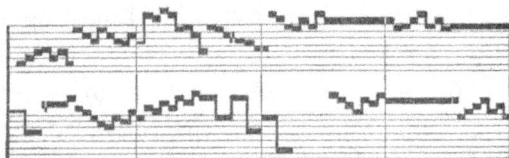

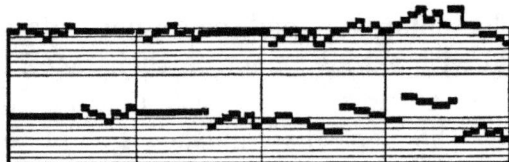

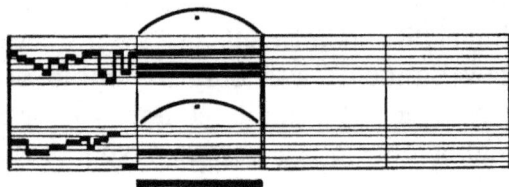

[1]"Probably," replied Uncle Phil, "you were more interested in seeing my fingers wiggle than in listening to the music, weren't you?" And turning to Jack, "And you, probably, did not get the text. Naturally it would sound like a jumble of noises, unless you knew the little melody out of which the whole piece was made.

"Before playing it again let me tell you about this piece. It is by a composer who lived a long time ago, named Johann Sebastian Bach, and he called it a 'Two-part Invention.' This is number one. You see how different the name is from those of the other pieces that I played to you. You remember the 'Boat Song' and the 'Spring Song' and 'The Wild Rider.' This name, 'Two-part Invention,' is merely a description of how the composition is put together, and does not tell you anything of what the imagination, or make-believe, should do. The reason for this is that the fun we get out of this music is more in noticing the way it is made than in using the imagination as we did with the Schumann and Mendels-

[1] See the preceding diagram of the Invention drawn to scale both as to duration and pitch. The initial figure in the upper part is the text of the piece. It appears upside down at the beginning of the third measure and, with the addition of a single note between the figures, forms a continuous run of two measures. The same occurs for the lower part at the beginning of the third measure of the third brace.

sohn pieces, though of course we can imagine all we want and play with the piece in the same way, too. 'Two-part,' in the name of this piece, means that there are two voices, or parts, as in a duet when two people sing at the same time. 'Invention' means that the composer tried to see in how many ways the little subject at the beginning of the piece could be worked in. That is to say, he was going to show his skill in inventing every possible combination of the little melody. You have been to ball games and enjoyed intensely the clever way in which some player got out of a fix or succeeded in getting beyond or out of reach of the man who was playing against him. So in this kind of music, our main interest is in watching the game and seeing how the old composer's inventiveness managed to use the little melody and have it all good music at the same time. I assure you that's no easy stunt, and the harder the music the greater the fun in listening to it, if we can follow the way it was done.

"Let me play this little melody to you over and over so that you can remember it."

Their uncle played over the two measures, pointing with one hand to the notes so that the children could make a connection between the sound and the appearance of the notes.

"Now then," he said, "see if each of you can hum the little text to me."

Neither of the children did it correctly, and after laughing at their slowness, their uncle gave them a chance for a little more practice. He then played the piece again, and both children were surprised to find that what seemed like mere rapid finger work and a jumble of sounds had at least strains in it that were quite rational.

"How many times do you think this little text comes in these two pages?" asked Uncle Phil.

"About four or five times, I guess," said Jack. Nell nodded assent. Their uncle smiled. "It comes in, if I am not mistaken, thirty-seven times, and the difference between the four or five times that you have heard and the thirty-seven times that it does come in, shows you how much of the game you have lost."

This challenged Jack's attention. "Try it again," he said.

"Before I do that," replied his uncle, "let me play parts of it here and there, that you may see if you can discover the little text."

"Why, that sounds like it, but I don't know where it begins or where it ends."

"Look here," said Uncle Phil; "I am pointing to the little run that is made up by the addition of only a single note, between two repetitions of the melody." Then he played another one that also reminded them of the text, but neither child could tell why.

"Let me show you where the notes are," said their uncle, "and you look carefully, first at them, and then at the way it was printed at the very beginning, and see if there is anything that is alike in the appearance of the two."

"Oh," said Nell, "it's just like the first, except that it is upside down. It goes on over and over in the same way."

"Who would have thought of that !" said Jack.

"That's where the invention comes in," said Uncle Phil. "Now I will play the whole piece over very slowly, and you watch the notes and at the same time listen, and see if you can follow the game."

The children braced themselves for the concentrated effort while their uncle played the invention, taking special pains to emphasize the theme wherever it came in.

"Isn't that fun?" cried Nell.

"Why, there's almost nothing else but the little melody in the whole piece."

"Wasn't the old composer clever to be able to do that? Now you go off where you cannot see me playing or see the music and just listen while I play it again. Does it sound like a jumble of noises now?"

"No, not at all," said Jack. "But you have got to know the rules of the game if you are going to get any fun out of it."

"True, in a sense," replied Uncle Phil; "you would get a lot more fun out of it if you knew all the rules that the composer had to follow in writing this bright little piece, but that would be asking too much from the ordinary listener. The piece has become much more interesting to you, simply because you have learned the text and are able to follow it in the clever turns it takes. All you have really done is to pay attention and remember what you have heard. And you see how important attention and memory are for appreciating this sort of music. But while pieces like the one I have been playing demand the closest attention and memory, every piece that is worth hearing at all requires attention and memory in order that we may enjoy it as much as it deserves.

"You see now that listening to music is very much more than merely hearing the sounds as an animal might. First of all we must hear good music in order to have something for which to listen. By good music I don't mean music that just you or someone else likes, but the kind of music that has been enjoyed by a great many intelligent people for a long time. In other words, music that has proved its value in just the same way that a boy proves to be a good fellow — he is one that not only all the decent fellows like, but that they like right along and don't get tired of after a few weeks.

"Besides having good music, what else must we do?"

"Pay close attention to what we hear," Jack answered promptly.

"Yes," added Nell, "when we hear a song we must listen to the words as well as to the music, so as to understand the 'make-believe' of the music, like the galloping horse."

"But what do you do when there are no words, as in a piano piece?"

"You still 'make believe,'" she answered.

"Yes," added Jack, thinking of the examples. "Unless you pay attention you can't understand the music, especially the last kind that made you listen so hard to remember what you heard."

"Those are good answers," said Uncle Phil. "Some day I will play you more music and review these points. Now you will have to go out and play hard enough to make up for lost time."

The children rushed out, but not feeling at all that the hour with their uncle had been lost.

Section 4

The children's mother, who had been an interested listener, at once exclaimed:

"I never realized before how important the hearing of good music is. It not only forms our tastes, but it establishes our habits of listening."

"Very true," replied her brother, "music in this respect is like literature. If we constantly read poor works depending for interest on sensationalism and excitement rather than on truth and beauty, we not only form a taste for poor literature, but we also form bad habits of reading and listening. In music this is even more serious, for while the necessities of daily life require us to use language so that we are able at least to understand what is said in good literature, even if we do not like it, in music we have so little experience that after we have heard poor music for a while — especially in early childhood — we are unable even to listen intelligently. Under such conditions good music sounds stupid and dull instead of interesting."

"I am also very much impressed," said his

sister, "by the way you set my children to listening. I never should have dared to try such instrumental pieces with them, and yet they were intensely interested. In fact," she added, "I was so interested myself, that the old 'Invention' that I used to dislike when I had to practice it, sounded like a fascinating gem."

"Yes," he answered, "so much depends on the point of view. I was following a fundamental educational principle, giving the children something to do with their attention — something to look for — setting a problem as a challenge, rather than just telling them to exercise it."

"Have you other suggestions for interesting my children in music?" asked his sister.

"There are two more points that it would be well to consider; one is to have them reproduce, and the other to describe what they hear. With reference to the first, reproduction, children, especially little ones, are so interested in doing things, that an ingenious mother or teacher can have them hum, sing, or whistle the tune, or clap the rhythm of fragments of fine compositions, telling what they are from. For this purpose good music should be selected, and seldom the whole of a composition. For instance, take the first part of the

slow movement of Haydn's 'Surprise Symphony'
and let the children memorize the fascinating
nursery tune with which it starts. They are
always fond of Haydn's little joke, the un-
expected crash of the big drum that makes
everybody jump. At the same time, one must
never forget what a task it is to hold in mind
an instrumental composition of even five minutes in length. By taking a little at a time
and giving opportunity to reproduce the melodies of which the composition is made, the
child is prepared to take keen delight in the
whole. A few such works thoroughly enjoyed
are sufficient basis for the appreciation of
much classical music.

"The other point is to describe in words
what we hear. This is more for older children.
In fact, when the description is written, it
makes a good high school or even college exercise in English composition. It involves the
same principle as the previous point, that of
focusing the attention by giving the mind
something to do. Haven't you noticed, Helen,
that the good times you have described to
your friends, or written about, tend to fix
themselves in your memory? You have been
at dinners where the last funny story has.
driven the ones before out of your mind, but
if you are fortunate enough to repeat one of

E

these stories it then becomes a part of your repertory and more or less at your call. In other words, experiences which we have described to others tend to become part of us, while those that have been remembered only as states of pleasant or unpleasant feeling, fade away. The application of this to music requires that the composition heard be personified, giving the person's character, activity, and environment. This helps focus what is said.

"For instance, the piece may be gay. We can describe it as being the gayety of a child rather than of an adult, of a girl rather than of a boy; still further, it may be boisterous, or thoughtful and imaginative. When you consider the possible range of age, sex, and occupation, there is not a mood of music that may not be paralleled by such description. This, of course, does not mean that the music heard meant this to anyone else, but, as when looking at sunset clouds you are able to imagine certain shapes which for a moment others agree with you are resemblances, so you are able to discern the moods of the music thus personified. This is a very stimulating exercise for the imagination, and induces the most intense listening in the effort to catch and describe the mood. There is a creative element in such description

that makes the effort fascinating and at the
same time brings out our descriptive powers
along the important line of developing the
imagination and helps greatly in our education.

"These suggestions for guiding attention by
reproducing and describing, as well as those
you saw me illustrate with the children, are
all intended to help in listening to a kind of
music that demands more than does the popular
music of the day.

"But," continued Uncle Phil, "we must
remember that we cannot always live on the
plane of the great composers; we need a great
deal of music of the lighter sort, more to divert
us than to stimulate us to noble thoughts and
deeds, just as children need a kind of imaginative literature like 'Mother Goose,' or the
'Five Little Peppers,' and 'Alice in Wonderland'
— things so simple that they can be enjoyed
without effort, when heard. So there is a great
deal of light music which should have a place
in the musical life of the child. The point I
wish to make is the fact of the difference between these two kinds of music — a difference
which creates the necessity for two kinds of
listening. Either side of these two proposi-
tions may be overemphasized. You have seen
children brought up entirely with grown people,

on literature so far above a child's taste that
they seemed like prigs, without that childish-
ness that we are so fond of, though this type is
comparatively rare. The large majority make
a mistake the other way, taking only what
immediately appeals to them, without any
effort at careful listening. Those receiving
such training in music grow up with an exceedingly one-sided attitude towards the subject;
and while high school and college may do something for a few, the large majority are likely
to be hopelessly lost as far as enjoying worthy
music is concerned."

"Are you referring to music students?"
said his sister.

"Yes, but this is a problem not limited to
those who study music, for such people often
have their tastes improved through practice;
but it is also for the large public whose interest
in music is almost entirely one of appreciation. If this capacity has been injured by
hearing nothing but sensational music, such
people are, from the point of view of æsthetics,
ill, and need attention and care to develop a
wholesome taste. They are, to carry out my
illustration, too weak to profit by the music
that would do them good without a tonic in the
form of help for concentrating attention.

"The need for guidance and help has become

urgent since the great increase in the possibility of producing music in the home by means of disks and rolls. The opportunity for hearing music has gone beyond any power of estimate. It would be difficult to say whether the total influence is, at present, good or bad, though I have no doubt that eventually this increase of our power to hear music will be considered as great in the realm of æsthetics as was the increase in the power to read, due to the printing press, with reference to general intelligence.''

"You are making me realize," said his sister, "what a responsibility rests on my shoulders with reference to the use made of our talking machine. I have thought of it only as an instrument of entertainment and have let the children do about as they please with it. I see now that it is molding their tastes as almost nothing else is.

"If I could put your suggestions towards listening into practice by the aid of nothing more than this instrument I might develop in the younger members of my family that interest in music that I have been longing for so much. I have been expecting schools and teachers to do this for them, while I neglected the most effective means for accomplishing what I wanted. Worse still, I have been allowing this powerful influence to be exerted on the wrong side. Yet, in spite of my musical training, I am at a loss how to select good material."

"Suppose," replied her brother, "we take this question up later as one of the important problems in music. People think they can get a list of things to hear which is to relieve them of all responsibility for exercising their own power of choosing wisely, forgetting that the valuable thing in the whole matter is to induce one really to exercise his own judgment. In other words, they trust aids in music as they do patent medicines."

"I see," replied his sister, "you don't intend that I shall throw off any of my responsibility. I shall certainly try to do better. Let me see if I remember all of your suggestions. First, that music is an expressive art and when it is employed with anything requiring the use of words, such as poetry, we should do our utmost to understand them in order to get the meaning of the music. Second, that music is an art that appeals to the imagination; unless we have our 'make-believe,' as my little girl says, very active when listening, we miss the spirit of the music. Third, that music is an art of design; beautiful forms are woven together, for the recognition of which it is essential that we remember what we hear.

Fourth, the most effective aid in grasping the tone, or form side of music, is to commit to memory the leading themes upon which the composition is constructed. And fifth, the most effective aid in grasping the mood, or content of the music, is to describe it in some dramatic way."

"Very good," said her brother. "You see from the list that the five heads have nothing to do with the technical aspect of music. They deal only with our power of enjoying music by listening."

"Why should not some capacity along these lines be considered as a requirement for the serious study of music?" asked Mrs. Brown. "For instance, I feel that if the children had been tested at school with reference to these five points they might have done much better work in actual study there. If the teachers had made sure that there was some general musical experience which these tests would have indicated, their teaching would have been much more effective."

"That is true! Teachers are now constantly taught that experience is the basis of instruction, but many go on teaching mechanically, without the slightest attempt to discover the basis of what they are teaching in the experience of the pupil. It is so much easier to do routine work than to treat each child as an individual according to his needs. In fact, our school system was not planned for such service, while the home, the most effective place for such work, seems to be neglecting it, expecting the over-loaded schools to do the whole training. Fortunately teachers are being better prepared for their work. If mothers could be as well prepared, many a child would be saved from a dull mediocrity, and society enriched by the service of developed talents."

"You do persist in rubbing it in," replied his sister. "If I had known what I do now, how much I might have done for the musical training of my children, long before they commenced school, by seeing that they were hearing plenty of attractive music of the good sort, with none of the bad, and listening to it more and more in the right way!"

"We are learning the importance of care in food for the body," said her brother, "and the method of conserving it; yet the sights and sounds that form the food of the mind we leave to uneducated nurse girls.

"I think," he continued, "we are agreed on the fundamental importance of musical experience as the basis of all systematic study. 'How to listen to music so as to enjoy it most keenly,' should be the first chapter of a musical education.

"We are ready now to take up the first problem of how to study notation without awakening a disgust for the subject. That problem is presented by your small boy. Send him to the studio, some time soon, and let me see if I can help him."

CHAPTER III

HOW TO LEARN NOTATION WITHOUT AWAKENING
A DISLIKE FOR MUSIC

Section 1

IT was arranged that Jack should call at the studio two afternoons a week, and he had willingly consented, as he had been much attracted by the music at the Thanksgiving gathering. One afternoon a vigorous ring at the door bell announced to his uncle that he had a lively little colt on his hands to guide in the straight and narrow path of musical accomplishment. The boy came into the room with rather a quizzical look on his face, evidently wondering what kind of ordeal he was to be put through to make him like his hated subject. He expected to be made to do something, and was most agreeably surprised when his uncle suggested singing to him.

"Oh," said the lad with enthusiasm, "sing that soldiers' song that you sang Thanksgiving day."

"Let me try a different one," said Uncle Phil, " and you see if you don't like it just as well."

Jack expected something about spring or robins, or perhaps a love song, and was surprised to have his uncle start in on a sailor song, "O Johnny, Come to Hilo." With each return of the phrase, "O Johnny, Come to Hilo, O Poor Old Man," his uncle pretended to be hauling on a rope. The vigor and go of the song so appealed to Jack that without knowing it he found himself imitating the motions and joining in the refrain. Then his uncle told him how the sailors used to sing while hauling on a rope, and how he had heard them sing on sailing vessels while hoisting the topsail yard.

"Now," said his uncle, "why do you suppose sailors sing while they work? Is it just because they like the music? Did you ever hear farmers singing in the fields or gangs of men working on buildings?"

Jack was puzzled. It certainly was strange why sailors sang while they worked. "Tell me, then," said his uncle, "why do soldiers have music while they are marching?"

"Oh," said Jack, "that helps them to keep step." Then his face lit up. "I know why sailors sing. It helps them to pull together."

"Exactly," said his uncle. "Can you tell me what it is in music that makes sailors pull together and soldiers march together?"

Jack felt that it was perfectly obvious that

music did help them, but he was perplexed to know how to express it.

"Well," said Uncle Phil, "you know we have to listen to a melody one sound after the other, so that we have to take time to hear the whole tune. We never can heàr it all at once the way we see a picture all at once. And because music takes time we have to connect what we have heard in the first part of the tune with what we are hearing later, or else, instead of getting the tune, we get only a succession of unrelated sounds. When I sang the sailors' song, you didn't have to hear it more than once, to know when the refrain was coming in. The reason why you are able to do so suggests the reason why sailors can pull and soldiers can march to music. It is because music is so planned that the sounds we sing one after the other all fit together like a block puzzle game, but instead of the blocks being made of wood as in the game, they are made of time lengths, each the same size."

"How funny!" said Jack.

"Yes," said his uncle, "and as soon as you have heard the tune you know what all these time lengths are. For instance, in the sailors' song, you know just when to haul, because the pattern of the tune just fits the time lengths. As long as you know the tune, you know what the right time is either to step or to pull. Now, when you make music in school, do you know of anything that you do that takes the place of stepping and pulling?"

Jack thought for a moment and then with an inquiring look, asked, "Does the beating time, down, left, right, up, mean the same as the pulling of the sailors?"

"That's it!" said his uncle. "Your down, left, right, up, has to go with sections of the tune and makes you feel the time parts of the tune in the same way that sailors and soldiers do.

"Can you tell me whether it makes any difference where you start with the first down? In other words, are there some places in the tune that should be down, and some up? Let's try 'O Johnny, Come to Hilo.' When is the best time to say 'down'?"

"When you pull down," said Jack.

"And what do you do when the 'up' comes?"

"You get ready for the next pull."

"Exactly so," said the uncle. "The down, left, right, up, of the tune means four different places in the motion of the tune. The 'down' is where you step or pull, and the 'left' is where you get ready for the next, and sometimes you can pull, or step, on the 'right,' and sometimes you wait until the 'up' is past before you pull or step again.

"Why do you suppose your teacher wants you to beat the time when she says 'down, left, right, up,' as you sing? Is it because she wants to be disagreeable and make you try to think of two different things at the same time?" Jack colored a little, because he remembered that that had been his idea, at least in part. "Are they really two different things," continued his uncle, "or are the singing and beating time parts of the same thing? Did you feel that they were separated in the sailors' song, or the soldiers' march?"

"No," said the lad, "they are one." Then his face lighted up. "I never tried to think of them as going together. Beating time was one thing and singing a tune was another for me."

"Now," said Uncle Phil, "what are you going to do next time you sing some new music?"

"I must think of them as one."

But he was unable to say how the down, left, right, up should fit the music so as to make them one.

"How did you know when to pull in the chantey, or sailors' song?" asked his uncle.

"I listened to the music," said Jack, "that told me when to pull."

"Yes," said his uncle; "and so if you listen to the next song you sing, and remember that

the down beat is the one at which you pull or
step, you will find that the tune will tell you
just when to beat down, left, right, up.   In fact,
some tunes will tell you to say down and up,
and some will say down, right, up."

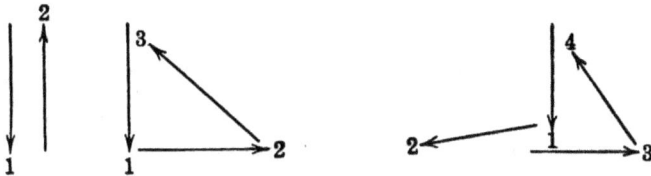

Two, three and four time beats.

"Why down, right, up?" asked Jack.

"Because," said his uncle, "after the down
beat there are only two beats that are weak
before the next strong down beat comes, and
so musicians mark the difference in beating
time between four and three part music, by
making the second beat in three part time go to
the right, instead of the left.   In this way you
will remember to go up, and have the hand
ready to go down on the next pulse, or accented
part of the tune."

"I see," said the lad.   "I hope we have a
chance to do some of it the next time we sing
in school, for now I think I can do it."

"That's right," said his uncle, "we should
test what we learn.   Let me make sure before
you go, however, that you have a clear idea of

what you would do about this question of
beating time. Do you remember the illustration of music's being like a picture puzzle
where one puts the blocks in the right place,
by noticing the way the picture goes? Music
is divided into equal time lengths, which is the
reason why we can march to it, but these lengths
are not all accented alike. If they were, we
never would know which foot to start off with.
But there is always one strong one, which is
the one you have to look out for; in some pieces
the strong accent is followed by one weak accent,
and in some with two weak accents, and in some
with even three weaker ones, before the strong
one comes in again. Beating time with the
hand is only one way to help yourself to keep
track of all this, and if the music doesn't make
your hand go with it, so that the two are one
thing, it's no use to beat the time."

"That's so," joined in Jack, so emphatically
that he brought a smile to his uncle's face.

"Good," said Uncle Phil. "I am glad you
have the point that beating the time is only
to help you feel the time parts more definitely,
and that it is a very silly business to be swinging
your hand about while singing, if it is not to
some purpose. In fact, one should drop all
such aids as soon as possible. It's like using a
crutch, very helpful when needed, but harmful

when not needed.   Some good teachers do not teach beating time, but make the student feel the time parts in other ways."

This explanation pleased Jack, for it appealed to his common sense, while what he had been doing in school had seemed childish.   He was all the more anxious to test his knowledge.

Section 2

In the next lesson, his uncle drew attention to the fact that while the hand was beating "down, left, right, up " in an even way, the sounds that went with it were sometimes fast and sometimes slow.   They tried the same chantey again, this time trying to watch how the tones of the tune went with the motion of the hand. · Jack was very much interested, for he found a new fact to observe.   Then they tried "Yankee Doodle."   He was interested to see that the tones of the tune went twice as fast as the motion of the hand, perfectly regularly.

"What does this remind you of in connection with the musical puzzle I spoke of last lesson?" asked Uncle Phil.

"I know," answered Jack instantly.   "You compared the regular beats of music with the regular squares.   The different way the music goes must be the picture on the squares."

F

"That's right," said Uncle Phil, "sometimes there is more than one object on the square, and sometimes there are a number of squares covered by one object, in the same way that there are sometimes more than one tone to a beat and sometimes there are a number of beats to one tone.

"That puzzle example works well, does it not?" went on Uncle Phil. "You have ob-

Illustration of meter signature.

served two very important things in music; the regular time lengths, called beats, or pulses, and the free flowing motion of the music, showing how a particular piece goes. Can you tell me now how this irregular free design in music can be represented so it will fit the regular beats?"

Jack had never thought of this problem, and he puzzled considerably over it. "What would show you that the sounds of 'Yankee Doodle' were going twice as fast in proportion to your hand as 'America' goes most of the time? To put it in the form of your picture puzzle, — 'Yankee Doodle' needs two sounds in each time square, while 'America' needs but one most of the time. The question is, how is this shown in the notes?"

Suddenly an idea flashed into Jack's mind. He remembered the musical arithmetic that had been such a bore to him, and he said, "Does the way it is shown have anything to do with quarters and eighths and the rest of it that we have in school?"

"Certainly," said his uncle. "'America' is written in quarter notes and 'Yankee Doodle'[1] in eighths, and as there are two eighths in a quarter, if the tones in 'America' went at the rate of your hand, then those in 'Yankee Doodle' would go twice as fast."

This was the first time that the fractions in music had meant anything to Jack. He realized what he never had before, that the entire confusing lot of whole, half, quarter, eighth, and sixteenth notes, and the rests that are like them, were merely to help the composers make their

[1] Originally, "Nankee Doodle," dating from the time of Cromwell, played first by English troops in derision of the Yankee Continental Army. The jolly tune made friends and was adopted, and is now a national air.

musical designs fit the regular pulse of the
music. This threw a flood of light on what had
seemed a meaningless application of arithmetic
to music.

"Now," said his uncle, "can you show how
the musicians tell in print the way you should
beat the time over and over, — whether one,
two, three, four; or one, two; or one, two,
three?"

Again a bit of old experience came back to
him, and the boy said, "Does the figure on the
staff, at the beginning of the music, have something to do with it?"

His uncle drew a staff on a piece of paper.
"Do you mean these figures?" he asked, placing
the metrical signature.

"Yes," said Jack.

"Tell me what these two figures mean," continued Uncle Phil (see p. 66). "Why are those
for 'Yankee Doodle' different from those for
'America'?"

But Jack could not say. Finally his uncle
helped him by saying, "Sing the tunes over to
yourself, and pick out where the down beat
comes."

The boy's face brightened, for he felt the
two-meter rhythm of "Yankee Doodle" against
the three of "America." He saw that the
upper figure of the signature in "Yankee Doodle"

was two, and in that of "America," three, and he said, "These are the figures that show you how the tunes must go."

"What then," asked his uncle, "does the lower figure mean which is alike in both tunes?" This was a puzzler. "If I wanted to tell the size of this book, what would I have to do?"

"You would measure it."

"What would I do if I measured it?"

This seemed a foolish question. "Why," said Jack, "you would tell me how many inches long and how many inches wide it is."

"Then," said his uncle, "are you giving me the measurements of the tunes when you are telling me only how many beats there are in each tune? If I should say the book was eight one way and six the other, would you know what the size of the book was?"

"I can guess," said Jack.

"What would you add to the figures to tell the size?"

"Inches. They couldn't be eight feet."

"No," said his uncle, "nor eight miles. So in these tunes, when you said one had three beats and one had two beats, what would you have to add to tell me what the length of the beat is?"

He noticed the signatures 3.4, and 2.4 (see p. 66). He remembered that "Yankee Doodle" went twice as fast as the hand. A happy guess flashed in his mind. "The lower number must mean what kind of a note each beat of the hand goes to."

"Yes," said Uncle Phil. "And in these two tunes they were both quarter notes. The lower number in the fractions of the signatures must then mean the length of the beat.

"Next time you come I am going to play to you and have you show me whether you really know what we have been talking about."

The idea of hearing some music pleased Jack, though he was a little fearful whether he would be able to answer his uncle's questions.

Section 3

It was but a few days later after school, that Jack came again to the studio. He expected some questions, but instead his uncle played the vigorous "Soldiers' Chorus" from Gounod's "Faust."

"Would this be a good piece to play when you wish to put the baby to sleep?" he asked.

Jack laughed at the idea and said, "No, that sounds as if soldiers were marching, and they felt jolly and victorious."

"That is just what it is," said his uncle, "it is a soldiers' chorus from a great opera. Do you suppose you could march to it?" Jack thought that he could. "If you can march to it, you can tell me all about the measure, can't you?"

Jack was surprised to find that by making his hands go with the tune he easily found the "one, two, three, four."

"Now," said his uncle, "let me play you another piece. What does this sound like?"

Jack thought it sounded like a lot of people singing together, and while they were not marching gayly like the soldiers in the previous piece, he still could not help stepping to the movement as it swung along. He found no difficulty in getting the down or accented beat, but was perplexed when it did not fit the pattern of the previous one, for the accent came first on one foot and then on the next.

"Can't you tell me about that?" said his uncle. "You remember when the stepping or pulling part of the tune came, the other day, you always said *down?* Now let us see how these down steps follow each other."

Jack tried again, and immediately realized that this must be three part time, for the downs came after two steps instead of three, as in the march.

"This," said his uncle, "is the 'Pilgrims' Chorus'[1] from 'Tannhäuser,' an opera by

[1] The "Pilgrims' Chorus" is published in most high school song books and may be obtained for both the piano player and phonograph.

Richard Wagner." Then he described a little
of the scene that occurs when the " Pilgrims'
Chorus" is sung. Jack wanted to hear bits of
both pieces again. Not only was his imagination stirred with the pictures that his uncle
suggested, but he felt that he could see into the
music. It was not just a collection of sounds,
but they were arranged; and when he wished
to, he could tell what the arrangement was.
His uncle continued, "How long a note does
this ' Pilgrims' Chorus ' start with?"

The boy had never thought of such a thing
before, and said, "How can I tell?"

"How could you tell if I should ask you how
long that desk was?"

"I should measure it."

"What would you measure it with?"

"A rule."

"What would you need to have marked on
your rule in order to tell me just the size of the
desk?"

"Inches."

"Would the inches have to be all alike?"

"Certainly," smiled Jack.

"Then to measure a length you would need
something with regular spaces on it. Didn't
you find something that went regularly in the
sailors' song, and in the soldiers' song, and in this
piece that I played to you to-day (see p. 66)?"

"Yes," said the boy, "the steps, or the beating of time, went regularly, while the tones were sometimes long and sometimes short."

"Then all you have to tell me about the first tone in the 'Pilgrims' Chorus' is to say how it compares with the beat."

"Try it again," said Jack, "and let me see. Oh, that is only one beat long."

"How long is the next sound?" Uncle Phil played the music while Jack beat the time.

"I gave two beats to the second note, then one to the next."

"You seem to have no difficulty in measuring off the sounds."

"No," said Jack, "but you have to listen very hard."

"That's true," said his uncle. "That is just the use of this sort of work. It makes you listen and you get keen in doing so. Of course, this would help you also to read and write music, and you might not want to do much of that; but you would always want to enjoy music, and the more you could hear in the music the more you would enjoy it. This practice in telling how the music goes and in listening to music is like getting your muscle up in the gymnasium for a game. Of course, you can enjoy music without knowing anything about it, in the same way people enjoy flowers

and birds without knowing their names. But
the people who know the names and habits of
birds and flowers always see more of them, and
that is how knowing helps you in music."

The boy went off delighted with his music
lesson. When he got home he told his mother
about the famous pieces he had heard, and
how he could tell whether the music had three
beats or four beats in a measure, and how long
the tones were.

"Now, Mother," he said, "you sing 'Yankee
Doodle' and I will show you how to measure
the time of the tune."

His mother was delighted with Jack's enthusiasm, and said, "I don't see but that you are
doing the same kind of thing that you were
doing in school. What makes you like this
and hate what you did there?"

"Why," said Jack, "I understand how the
thing goes now. You see, in school we learned
to beat, 'one, two, three, four,' with exercises
that did not sound like music, so that I could not
make my hands go right when we had regular
music. But Uncle Phil made music first, and the
music made you go 'one, two, three, four,' and
all you had to do was to find out how the music
was making you go. You see, Mother, I don't
think I ever listened to music with my mind
before to-day. I never knew what to think of."

A shrill whistle sounded outside, the signal that his chum was waiting for him, and off went Jack. He had left much for his mother to think of with reference to learning notation. Above all, she realized that it made a big difference how the facts of notation were presented. Jack had had them in school as arbitrary items of information to be memorized, the reasons for which were to be understood later. Now these same facts were approached through music, so that the causes which produced them were obvious, thus enlisting his reason in mastering the facts, and not only making the work both interesting and effective, but also developing in the pupil the power to solve his own problems, which is the most important training that the school can give. It seemed to this practical mother, as she thought over her children's work, that formal education appeared to make the pupils' work a mere matter of mechanical memory, with as little use of reason as possible. At the same time she realized how in her own treatment of her children she was inclined to do the same thing, not because she did not appreciate the rational approach, but simply because the other was easier and seemingly quicker of accomplishment.

Section 4

At Jack's next lesson his uncle's first question was, "How did your new knowledge work? Did you have a chance to try it?"

"Fine," replied Jack. "I did have a chance. I first listened as hard as I could to the music, looking out for the strong beats, and when I was sure, I filled in the weak ones. This gave me something to measure with. The next thing I did was to try it on, so when the school was singing the tune again, I kept my measuring going steadily and listened how the tune went. I am sure that in the chorus I could tell what kind of note to write for every tone sung."

"That is fine," replied his uncle. "You are well started towards mastering the two great problems in music. The first, musicians call the metrical aspect of music. It has to do with the measuring of the time that the music occupies. The second shows how a given tune fits in with the time of the meter. Some musicians call this the rhythm of the music. Meter, then, shows with what we measure, and rhythm, what is measured. There is a third problem that I want to tell you about to-day. This, with the two you have, will give you the foundation of music. The one for to-day is not only hard to observe but very hard to put into notation;

so give your best attention, and tell me when I play something different."

His uncle started out gayly playing " Yankee Doodle " with one hand. Then he commenced to sing it in another key, but much lower.

"Same thing," said Jack.

Uncle Phil then picked up his violin and fairly made the tune spin on the E string.

Jack laughed at the jolly change in the tune, and said, "It is always 'Yankee Doodle' wherever you play it."

"But," said his uncle, "I sang it with slow and big tones way down low; I played it higher up on the piano, and faster, and not so loud; and then I played it on the violin way up and very fast. Still you call them all 'Yankee Doodle.' Doesn't it make any difference whether the tone is low or high, loud or soft, fast or slow?"

Jack thought it did.

"I will play the same tune again, and introduce the same changes, but this time differently." He then played, changing the pitch of individual tones in the tune. Playing it again he changed the accents; the third time he changed the time lengths, making some tones faster and others slower. All these so altered the tune that the boy laughed.

"Can you tell me why differences in low or

high, loud or soft, fast or slow, did not make any particular difference in the tune in the first example, and spoiled it in the second?"

Jack thought it over. Why was it that the same changes when introduced uniformly through the whole tune made so little difference, while only a little introduced with a part of the tune made such a lot of difference? "It's a hard answer to put into words," said his uncle. "Let me give you a different kind of example."

He then took up a piece of paper, drew a square and then a circle, and then he repeated them in different sizes. "Do the sizes of these circles and squares have anything to do with the general appearance of the design?"

"No," said Jack, "one set are circles and the other set are all squares."

"Would they be different if I should use any different colored ink, or if I should mark them on the sand, or make them out of stone? One series would always be circles, and the other series would always be squares, wouldn't they? Then what is it that makes the circle design, and the square design, and the design which makes you always recognize 'Yankee Doodle'?"

Jack looked perplexed. It seemed impossible to say in words what was so obvious in facts.

His uncle asked, "Suppose I started out to make a small circle, but before completing it drew the line out to make a large circle, or if I treated the square similarly, making one side short and the other much longer, would they still remain circles and squares, or would they look different, and all out of proportion?"

"I see," said Jack, "what made 'Yankee Doodle' sound the same in the first examples, was because you kept the proportion the same, like the squares and circles, while in the second example you changed the proportion when you started out to make a small circle and changed to a large one in the middle."

"Good," said his uncle; "the third problem in music is also about the proportion of music; but instead of being the proportion of time and length of tone that you already know about, the proportions we are now going to study are those of the distance as it seems to us of one tone from the other. Musicians call it difference in pitch. In order to find out such distances we shall need a standard to measure with. We want to know how the proportions in pitch are used as we do those of time. Have you ever thought whether the *do, re, mi's* could possibly have anything to do with proportions? You know, having proportion means that its parts are related to each other. What is it that related the *do, re, mi's?*"

This was a new idea. Perhaps after all there was a way to measure how far the tones went up and down, as beating had measured the length of tones.

"Let us sing 'Yankee Doodle' and see if we can find one important tone from which all the others take their proportionate distances."

Jack hummed the tune through, reflectively, while his uncle strengthened the harmonic feeling by giving the chords softly.

"Might it be the first tone?" asked Jack.

"Does it come in anywhere else? You can keep humming this tone to yourself, very lightly, while I play the tune through at the piano."

"You kept hitting it over and over while you were playing the tune, and then you ended on it."

"That then must be the tone from which we measure the others," replied his uncle.

"Is the first tone always the measuring tone?" asked Jack.

"Sometimes tunes commence on other tones, but they cannot go far without making the measuring tone important, in the same way that a tune cannot go on without making you soon feel the pulse or beat, and making you march and pull with its swing. You had to observe carefully in order to tell how this pulse went. How did you carry on this observation?"

"I noticed how the tune made me feel inside when the pulling or marching tones came."

"In the same way you have to watch how you feel in order to discover the important measuring tone of the tune. Musicians call this note the key-note, or tonic, of the piece."

He then tried "America," and Jack could easily tell what the important or home tone was. Then his uncle hummed a little of "Suwanee River," and the boy tried to hold the first tone as the important one, but somehow it did not work right. After listening to the tune a few times he was sure it was the third note.

"You see," said his uncle, "it isn't so hard to tell if you watch for what you feel inside of you, and do not look for an object like a stick or a stone. Let me try some other tunes."

Jack in his eagerness was constantly getting the wrong tones, so Uncle Phil stopped and explained again, "What we are looking for is not in the sound, but is something that happens inside of you, and if you try to find it before it happens, you will just as likely not let it happen, because your attention, fixed on something else, will be in the way." It was very hard for Jack,

G

when he heard a new tune, not to jump at an answer, but instead, to wait and listen until he recognized the key-note of the piece. He found no difficulty in discovering it, if he waited patiently before he made his mind up. "After a while," said his uncle, "you will not have to wait so long to know, but now you must be very patient.

"We have found the key tone. Now let's start on it and sing the tones right up, in order, and see when it comes in again." This they did, Uncle Phil singing the tones while Jack counted.

"The eighth tone sounds exactly like the first one," he said.

"That's right," said his teacher, "and if we commence with these eight tones and go right up with another eight tones you will hear nothing that you have not heard before, except that it will sound higher. Or if we go down, it is the same, only lower. In other words, after every seventh tone, we commence the series over again. Then how many different tones will you have to learn?"

"Seven," said Jack.

"So that all you have to do in order to tell how such tunes go is to learn these seven tones, and one of them you have almost learned now."

"Well," said Jack, "I think if I listened to a

tune carefully enough, I could find out the key-note, but I never could tell the others."

"If you can find the key-note you can't very well help finding what the other six tones are, for that is only a matter of thinking it out. It is, however, difficult to do this unless you have some way of naming the tones. Names and words help us to keep in mind what we are thinking about. People have used various ways of naming tones; some have called them by numbers."

"Yes," broke in Jack, "Nell writes numbers on the staff instead of notes."

"Yes, and others use letters. For instance, the four tones that the four strings give on my violin are called by the letters, *g, d, a, e,* so that the strings are called by these names. As it is hard to sing letters and numbers, teachers have used still another set of names that, because they are convenient to sing, help us to connect the name and the sound."

"I never thought *do, re, mi,* was naming anything," said Jack; "how can you name just sounds?"

"You can't very well," said his uncle. "All that teachers want to do is to name the relations of the tones to each other, — in other words, 'do' does not stand for any particular pitch, but for the tone that sets the standard for the

others,—or, as we called it before, the home
tone. I am going to take up a similar naming
of the other six tones with you in a little while.
These names are sometimes called relative
names, because they show the connection of the
tones with each other, and do not stand for any
particular pitch.

"I want to tell you now, how long ago and
how very interestingly those names came to be
used. A very clever teacher taught an old pope
to sing from notes by the use of these names,
almost nine hundred years ago. At that time
they used to sing a hymn to St. John in Latin.
Each line of the hymn began on the tone above
the first tone of the preceding line. The way
this shrewd old teacher taught the pope was,
first, to teach him the tune, and when the tune
was thoroughly learned, he left off all of each
line except the first syllable. For instance, the
first syllable was *ut*, the second line commenced with the syllable *re*, the third line with
the syllable *mi*."

The lines of this hymn, written in the eighth
century, start on the successive tones of the
scale. In the early eleventh century the first
syllable of each line became the singing name of
a six-tone scale. About 1600 "si" was added
for the seventh tone and later, in most countries,
"ut" was changed to "do."

ut — quaent laxis   fa — muli tuorum
re — sonare fibris   sol — ve polluti
mi — ra gestorum   la — bii reatum
                   Sancte Johannes

"Oh! holy John! cleanse
from the guilt of polluted lip;
that thy servants may be able
to sound again with relaxed
chords the marvels of thy deeds!"

"That's almost *do, re, mi,*" said Jack.

"Exactly," said the uncle; "later teachers changed the *ut* to *do* and the old teacher, named Guido of Arezzo, that started this system, never went any farther than *la* with his names. Afterwards one was added called *ti*, some calling it *si*, and you have *do, re, mi, fa, sol, la, ti, do*, with *do* coming in again. Why do you suppose that old teacher taught the tune?"

"I don't know," said Jack.

"Because after the tune was thoroughly learned, the order of the syllables, although they made no sense, could easily be remembered. There would be no use in learning the syllables unless one knew exactly how they follow each other."

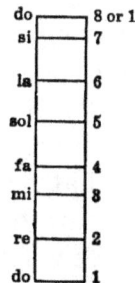

Diagram of the scale, sometimes called the tone ladder.

do	8 or 1
si	7
la	6
sol	5
fa	4
mi	3
re	2
do	1

"That's so," said Jack. "I do get so mixed up on the *do, re, mi's.*"

"Then the thing for us to do is to get them straightened out, isn't it," said Uncle Phil, "so we can use them for remembering the order of the tones? For after all their only use is to help the memory and to supply a name that will show the relation of the sounds to the key-note. If you were doing an arithmetic example and you could not multiply correctly, there would be no use in trying to do your example until you had learned the multiplication table, would there? You have been trying to do an example of the musical scale, without really knowing the order of the names — the very thing that was to help you tell the relation of the tones to the key-note.

"I think," continued Uncle Phil, "you have been trying to do too many things at once. What we need to do is to go slower. Let us separate the names from the sounds, and see first whether we can always know their positions and where they should go when the key-note is on different places on the staff. Then we will see if we can connect these names with the tones and thus measure the exact distances of the tones in our tunes. In other words, just as we know something about adding and subtracting, before we work examples in arithmetic, so we must know certain facts about the scale before we really try to solve our musical problems of note reading. You have learned already to recognize the key-note, and you know the first name, *do*. Can you tell me what the important things are that you have learned to-day?"

Jack remembered the illustration of the circle and the square, and said, "We have learned that what makes a tune is the proportion between its tones, shown by the distance of the tones from each other. Certain distances make certain tunes, and playing the tune loud or soft, high or low, makes no difference as long as the proportions are kept the same."

"Remember, too," said his uncle, "that the plan of the tune is always reckoned from one important tone, called the key-note. This key-note is called 'one,' and is generally sung *do*."

"Yes," said Jack, "because an old teacher made his pupil sing a tune that went up one tone of the scale for each line of the song, so that the singing of the tune helped him to remember the order of the tones. So we sing *do*, *re*, *mi* now to remember how the tones go."

"Capital," said his uncle; "next time I am going to find out how accurately you know the order, not of the tones, but of the names."

Jack went off feeling that he had some idea
of how to measure tones up and down by first
listening for the key-note, or *do*, and that he
might by practice tell it in most of the tunes
that he knew.

Section 5

At the next lesson Uncle Phil had a small
blackboard ready for his pupil.

"If *do* is on the first line, where would *re* be?"
he asked.

Jack almost put it on the next line, then
happened to think that spaces as well as lines
were used. After placing the eight successive
tones with *do* on the first line, Uncle Phil said:

"Now let us see how this order of notes comes
in relation to *do*. With *do* on the first line, *mi*
comes on the second, and *sol* on the third line,
and the upper *do* on the second space above the
sol. The same thing would be true with
reference to the other lines if *do* was on the
second line, — *mi* and *sol* would come on following lines above it, and upper *do* would come on
the second space above the line *sol* came on. On
the other hand, if we should put *do* on a space,
mi and *sol* would come on spaces above, while
do would be on the second line above the space
sol came on. Think well about the way that
mi, *sol*, and upper *do* change when the lower *do*

changes, and see whether you can answer this question.

"But first I want to review something we talked about at the last lesson. Are the sound names, the *do, re, mi's*, as they are called, the names of definite sounds in the same way that Charles is the name of one of your friends and Tom is the name of another; or are they names to show the relationship of tones to each other, in the same way that the third post in that fence out there makes you look at a definite post? The number three isn't the name of that post, is it?"

Jack puzzled quite a while on this question, because he did not grasp the significance of the relative names. He had thought that *do, re, mi* were the names of particular sounds, which should be always just the same, and from his uncle's inquiries, it looked very much as if they were not the names of particular sounds, but that they showed only the distance that they were from each other. *Re*, for instance, could not mean any certain tone, but merely the tone that was the distance of *re* from *do*. This was an interesting idea, for the boy had been trying all the fall to learn the sounds. Unfortunately he was in the habit of memorizing the relative names in connection with the lines and spaces upon which they come in a given key, so that when the key was changed he was confused. He had not thought that if the relative names stood for the relationship of tones to each other and not for a fixed pitch they must also change relatively on the staff.

"How is it, then," Uncle Phil went on, "that the tone that sounds like *do* in one piece sounds like another entirely different tone in a different piece? You sing or make the tones exactly the same."

The fact was obvious to Jack, but the explanation seemed impossible. The mere changing of the numbers given to certain things ordinarily made no difference in the things. For instance, if he had seven apples in a row on a table, he might count them one, two, three from either end, or start anywhere with one, without making any difference in the apples. But here were seven tones in a row, and the *do, re, mi* names were used as numbers. Yet if he started from any tone but *do*, nothing sounded right. He suggested this difficulty to his uncle.

"Let's try it," said Uncle Phil. Reaching to a dish on the table, he put eight apples before Jack and told him to arrange them in a row. Jack did so, and went through with his illustration, feeling quite confident of his reasoning. "You see," said Jack, "if we are calling these apples by number, it does not make any difference where I begin; but with the tones something different seems to happen."

"Yes," said his uncle, "you have before you a very peculiar fact. You remember that in the examples of the squares and circles, and of 'Yankee Doodle,' what made these designs was the way the parts fitted to each other. When we sing from *do* right up to the next *do* in order, we have what you might call a row of tones, or a scale. If the *do, re, mi* names are merely another way of numbering the tones, and *re, mi* merely mean the second and third tones in the series, then there ought not to be any difference where you commence to number one, any more than there would be where you commenced to number one with the apples. But it makes a big difference where we begin with the tones, because with them we are not merely numbering them so as to give their order, but we are doing much more, — we are telling their exact distances from each other. If I should place these apples with varying spaces between them, for instance, if the third and fourth, and the seventh and eighth apples were nearer together than the others, and we always wished to indicate by these numbers that the distances between these apples were smaller than between the others, then if we commenced on any other apple in the row than one, we should have to rearrange

the apples to make the short distances come between the right numbers."

"Do you mean," said Jack, "that *mi* and *fa*
are not just the third and fourth notes from *do*,
but that they are certain distances from *do*,
and from each other (see p. 85)?"

"Exactly," said Uncle Phil.

"And when we start on *do*, do we always sing
these same distances in going up and down the
scale?"

"Certainly, if we sing the scale correctly."

This was a great surprise to Jack, and he
wondered why, if he did such hard things while
singing the scale, he did not know it.

"But you do know it," said his uncle. "If I
sing the slightest bit out of the way, you feel
as if your teeth were set on edge; and if I
should sing some entirely different tone, you
would think that I was changing the order of
the scale. So you see, though you do not think
of distances when you are hearing a beautiful
tune, if any of the distances between the tones
of the tune were not exactly proportionate,
you would know it at once. Most people would
not think of it, however, as wrong distance;
they would merely say that it was the wrong
sound and call it a discord. In other words, the
do, re, mi, or sound names, while they are used as
equivalent to numbers, mean not only the first,

second, or third, in a series, but a particular distance for the first, and another particular distance for the second, and another particular distance for the third. Many teachers prefer to use the *do, re, mi* names instead of numbers, so that the student shall connect with each tone a quality due to its peculiar distance from *do*."

Section 6

"There is one more thing that I want to tell you about music, to-day. A piece of music is not like a picture that you can hang upon the wall and look at, all of it at once, but it is like a freight train passing the end of a street. You can get an impression of only a few cars at a time. The reason you can tell 'Yankee Doodle' from 'America' is that the tones, or in our illustration the cars, go by you in one order in 'Yankee Doodle,' and in another order in 'America,' so that music is always something that is going. It is a motion, and that is one reason why it is so hard to notice it; for as in the case of a train, when you are watching to see what the marks are on the first car, you miss the ones that come following after. If you did not care to notice anything, but just wanted to enjoy seeing them go flying by, you wouldn't have to bother about the number or the order.

You would just enjoy seeing them pass; and that is all we do in music when we take pleasure only in the motion. But when we study music so as to know how to read it and write it, we have to observe just how the tones follow one another, whether close together or far apart. In watching the train it would be the kind of cars that went by."

"What is the use of studying it," said Jack, "if we can enjoy it without that?"

"Because your enjoyment is greatly affected by such study," replied his uncle. "In learning the structure of music, how long the tones are in relation to each other, and how far they go up and down from the first note, you not only listen very hard, but also you remember. Practice in listening and remembering makes it possible for us to listen and remember more, and the more we listen and remember the more we get out of music. So learning about the tones makes it possible for us to enjoy music more.

"We have talked about proportions and distances of tones, and why we use names to tell them apart, and, in fact, why we study music at all. Now, before you go home, I want you to tell me how you will go to work to get some benefit from what we have been studying to-day."

"Well," said Jack, "I have got to learn how to measure the up and down of tones. The place we measure from is *do*, or the key-note, so I suppose the first thing for me to do when I wish to tell the tones of a tune is to find out which tone in the tune is *do* — the one from which all the rest are measured."

"Good for you.   Now for the practical question, how are you going to tell *do*? In 'Yankee Doodle' and 'America,' *do* is the first tone of the tunes; in 'The Star-Spangled Banner' it is the third, so you can't tell by the position of the tone."   Then continuing, he said, "Music gives the feeling of motion, like the passing of the train, and when the music stops the motion stops.   How does a tune make you feel when you are through with it, — as if you were going on, or as if you had stopped?"

"Oh," said Jack, "stopped, of course."

"Then, if you had been singing all sorts of skips, what tone do you think would be the most likely to make you feel satisfied, as if you did not want to measure any more distances, some tone that you had skipped to, or the measuring tone that we have already talked about, the one that is called the key-note, or tonic, to which we sing *do*?"

"*Do*, of course," answered Jack.

"Exactly.   Then all you need to do is to sing your tune through, and if it gives you the feeling of stopping completely you can be pretty sure that it is *do* you stopped on. Partial stopping places come often in the tunes, and *do* also comes in places where you do not stop. But if you get your last tone and keep it in your memory, while you are thinking the tune, you will pretty soon find that this *do* tone, in a short tune, seems to pervade the whole tune, and that in a lengthy one, the tone seems to go away from this *do* tone, but always comes back to it again, so that you feel that the tune has stopped. When you are by yourself, try over all the tunes that you can remember, and see if you can pick out the *do*."

That evening, when his mother asked Jack what he had been doing with his music, he described quite fully all that had been said with reference to measuring tones.

"First, there is music that one can dance and march to; you have to watch for the accented beat, for it tells you how the rest of the beats go. The second important thing is to find out how the time is divided up in the music you hear. You have to do this by measuring your tones with the regular time beats. The third thing is a hard one, for you have to measure the distances of tones from each other. Now, Mother," he said, "I wish you would sing a tune and let me see if I can find *do*."

She commenced to hum softly, " John Brown's

Body," or "The Battle Hymn of the Republic." The boy first thought that the beginning tone was *do*, so he gently hummed it to himself, while his mother went through the tune. It was very hard to keep this first tone, for it did not seem to match in well, and to his surprise the mother ended on a different tone. "Sing that last part of the tune once more, just before the chorus comes in." The repeated *do's* of the last phrase before the chorus gave him his cue. He asked her to repeat it two or three times until he felt sure he had found *do*.

"Now, sing it through from the beginning." He found this tone came in and was much easier to hold than the first tone he tried. It greatly pleased Jack to be able to work out such a step in music, for it made him feel that this subject — the hardest in all his school work — commenced to show some signs of rhyme and reason.

"I tell you, Mother," he said, "it makes you listen and remember, for when I do not keep repeating my *do* while you are singing the tune, I forget the tone I was looking for. It must show, Mother, that I have a weak memory for sounds. I must be somewhat like grandma, who keeps asking the same question over and over and forgets right away. But I know if I try a lot of tunes I can get so that I can remember and not have to keep asking you to repeat it."

H

Jack went on telling his mother of what
advantage it was to practice finding out the
names of the tones this way. "It improves the
musical memory, makes you get lots more fun
out of music; for Uncle Phil says that those
who listen and remember best are those who
can get the most out of music. I don't see
why we don't get more practice in school this
way. Lots of the facts you get in arithmetic,
history, and grammar, you could learn any time.
But learning to listen and remember what you
hear, is something you need practice in right
straight along. It isn't like reading something
out of a book, but it is like getting your muscle
up with training, and it takes time to train,
and the sooner you've got it, the more advantage you have right along. For you can use
your knowledge every time you are hearing
music."

"Quite true," said his mother, "and there is
something peculiar about music, different from
everything else. The faculty for listening to
music and remembering it is most easily cultivated when you are young. The earlier you
can do it the better. Almost all the great
musicians have been infant prodigies musically.
I hope you will work hard at your music so as
to make up for what you haven't had in the
lower grades."

"Don't you worry," said Jack; "I know more about *do* than most of the fellows now." |

The mother smiled with delight, not only because a hard subject was proving attractive, but also because confidence was coming with intelligence. She realized, as never before, the two important principles in teaching the study of notation: that first, the facts to be studied, named, and used, must be experienced in actual music. In other words, their real nature must be felt so that the study is about something as definite as when we study a bird, or learn how to make a sled; second, that the new things we learn in our study are selected for practical purposes, and to understand these reasons, what we study must be both intelligible and interesting. Finally, she realized the value of the analytic study of music, not merely as a means for mastering notation, but as a very important help in widening and deepening our capacity for enjoying music, through increasing our power of grasping what we hear.

CHAPTER IV

HOW A CHILD SHOULD LEARN TO SING

Section 1

JACK had done so well with his music that his mother decided to take his sister Nell to her uncle and find out whether he could help the child get a notion of what music really meant. The thought of going to Uncle Phil to see about her music delighted Nell. She felt confident that she would shine as she had in school. So when her uncle asked her to sing something to him, she was quite willing but could not think of anything. He repeated the title of a number of Mother Goose songs, and when he mentioned "Little Jack Horner"[1] she said, "I know that."

"All right, let's hear you sing it."

She started off a little excitedly and rushed through the tune catching her breath every third or fourth word, with apparently no more notion of rendering the thought than if the words were in a foreign language, whose meaning she did not know.

[1] Published in Mother Goose Series. Rhymes set to music by J. W. Elliot.

"Well," said Uncle Phil, "what is this song about?"

"Oh," she answered, "it isn't about anything. It is just a song."

"But," said her uncle, "my songs always tell a story. Don't yours?"

She commenced to think. "This song is about Jack Horner."

"What about him?"

"He stuck in his thumb and pulled out a plum."

"Where was he when he did this?" he asked her. He could see that the little girl was repeating the words over in order to get the connections.

"Now," suggested the teacher, "suppose you say the words of 'Little Jack Horner' to me." The Mother Goose picture book was placed before her to help recall the incidents of the words, and after a little practice in saying the words without the tune, she declaimed the whole situation of "Little Jack Horner," in a charming and effectively modulated voice.

"Now," said her uncle, "why don't you sing the song as you talk it? Tell first whom you are singing about, where he was, what he was doing, and what happened."

It was surprising to see what an intelligent phrasing was given to the tune as soon as the song was thought of as a story being told, through the tones of the melody, rather than as a melodic performance with the words as a non-essential hindrance.

"Let me sing you a song that my teacher taught me to sing when I was a very small boy," said Uncle Phil. He sang with a light voice the lovely folk song, "Sleep, Baby, Sleep."

The velvety softness of the pure and sustained vowel tones, and the fine articulation, had their mental effect on Nell, and she exclaimed, "Please sing it again!"

"Why do you want me to sing it again? I can tell you the story, about the little baby that was born with so many fine things to enjoy."

"Oh," said she, "I don't care to hear the story, I know that. But when you sing it, it seems almost as if I could see the little baby."

"Then you think there is a difference between singing and talking?"

"Of course," said she, "singing isn't talking, singing is fun."

"Well," said her uncle, "I'll repeat it and you tell me why it is fun."

Again the lovely melody and its adequate rendering had their effect. The bright eyes of the little girl listener showed her attention, but when the question came, "Why is sing-

ing different from talking?" the only reply
was, "It's more fun."

"I'll sing it once more to you," said her
uncle. "Tell me whether you still think it is
more fun."

The tune was now talked off somewhat as
one hears songs given in a variety show. Nell
laughed and said, "That sounds like a talking machine, it isn't as nice as when you sang
it first."

"Then, the difference isn't between talking
and singing," said Uncle Phil. "It is not just
singing, but singing in a way that is enjoyable,
for you liked one kind of singing and did not
like the other."

Nell nodded with vigor.

A new distinction about singing was coming
to her. She had always thought that singing
was singing, as much as talking was talking,
but evidently singing to be really fine must
not only do all that talking does, as she had
just learned, but something more, and a vague
feeling of what this something might be was
dawning on the little mind. "Do you remember," said her uncle, "how you sang 'Little
Jack Horner' to me a few minutes ago? And
how you sang it to me the first time? Which
of these ways do you think was the better, or
which way would you prefer to hear some-

body sing it to you? You said all the words, and sang the tune correctly both times.''

"The last way was much better," she said.

"What did you do to make the last way better? Was it just because you thought about what you were singing?"

There was an uncertain nod that showed that she was seeking for something more, and her uncle waited patiently for her to think it over. Her face suddenly brightened with an idea. She remembered how her teacher had said that they should sing with a sweet tone, and though she had no notion of what a sweet tone was, she felt now that the only difference between the two ways of singing "Little Jack Horner" must have been something in connection with the tone. This brought confidence, and although she could not describe tone quality, she felt that the last time she sang, the tune was sweet and beautiful, while the first time it was coarse and rough.

"Now," said her uncle, "the reason why you wanted me to sing the song over was not because you did not remember the story, but because you enjoyed the way I sang it. You liked the tune, and you remember you said that, when I sang it that way, you not only understood all about the little baby, but the singing actually made you see the beautiful baby in its fine home. That is just why we sing things instead of talking them. It makes the story beautiful, makes us like to hear it, and at the same time it makes it seem true and real. We call such singing beautiful. Tell me other things that you call beautiful. Is there anything on this table you think is beautiful?"

The little hand pointed to the roses, — "Those are beautiful."

"Anything else?"

The eyes wandered about the room and finally rested on a Royal Worcester vase on the mantelpiece. "That is beautiful," she said.

"Why do you call these beautiful? You don't call that coal scuttle beautiful, do you?"

"No." Yet she could not state why.

"It is a pretty hard question," said her uncle, "and I will help you. How do you think it would do to say that things which we love to look at are probably beautiful? You love to look at the roses, and that vase, but you don't care about looking at the coal scuttle, or the door mat, or the sidewalk. You love to look at the blossoms on the trees, and at the stars, and at a friend out there that is waiting for you — the big dog."

A vigorous nod of the head satisfied Uncle Phil that there was no doubt of the acceptance of this practical definition of beauty.

"Let us now return to our little tunes. The reason that you wanted me to sing the lullaby again was just because you enjoyed hearing the song as you enjoy looking at the roses. But when I sang the song with the rough talking kind of a voice, though it was correctly done, and the tune and the words were all the same, you only laughed, and you would have run away if I had kept on singing that way. Would there be any use in having the roses standing on the table if they were all wilted? You would know they were roses, but would there be any use in having them on the table?"

"Of course not," she replied.

"Then, unless the roses are beautiful, they are not worth having, are they? And that vase, if it were not beautiful, would not be worth keeping on the mantel, would it? It might do to put water in or something of that sort, but then we should put it in the pantry. The reason I keep it there is because it is beautiful. It is just the same with songs. If we wanted just to say things, we could talk the song a great deal better, but the song is like the roses, or the vase. Because it is beautiful we enjoy hearing it, and we don't care for it if it is not beautiful. When I asked you to sing 'Little Jack Horner' to me, did you sing it beautifully at first, or not?"

"I did not sing it beautifully," said Nell, rather sheepishly.

"Was there any use then in singing it?"

A thoughtful shake of the head showed that Nell was realizing the uselessness of the song, if it was not beautiful.

"What must you do in school when you are singing your song, besides remembering the tune and the words?" As the little pupil hesitated, her uncle helped her by saying, "Mustn't you sing them so that they are enjoyed? How do we describe what we enjoy singing, or hearing sung?"

"We say it's beautiful," said Nell.

"Then learning how to sing is learning how to sing beautifully, and just singing songs any way is not worth anything, is it? It is only when we sing songs so beautifully that we want to hear them again, that singing is worth while. Now, I want you to go home and tell your mother what we have to do in order to make singing worth while, and the next time you come we will try to find out how to make it worth while, or beautiful."

Section 2

When her mother questioned Nell as to what she had learned from her uncle, the child hesitated over the answer, for she had always thought of learning as repeating something she had memorized, and she realized, now, that though she had been some time with her uncle, she had not learned a thing in the way she had been accustomed to think of learning. And yet the long conversation with him had made an impression upon her. She thought over what had happened, of the two ways she had sung, and the two ways her uncle had sung, and she remembered the illustration of the wilted roses and the beautiful roses. Then she delighted her mother by saying,

"Mother, there are two kinds of singing. One is thinking of nothing but doing it correctly, and the other is singing so that people want to hear it again. Uncle Phil calls that beautiful singing. It makes you want to hear the tune over and over, in the same way that you want to look at roses."

"How did you sing to him?" asked her mother.

"When I first sang, I just sang the tune the way we do in school; I never thought of doing it any other way. Then Uncle Phil made me think of what I was singing about, and he said it sounded much better. But, Mother, you should have heard him sing 'Sleep, Baby, Sleep.' I wanted him to do it over and over. He said the reason why I wanted it again and again was because it was beautiful. I wish I knew how to sing beautifully."

Her mother was delighted that at last the self-satisfied little miss had awakened to the significance of the beautiful, and she pressed her daughter to her, and encouraged her by saying that that was just what her uncle was going to help her to learn to do.

When Uncle Phil came that evening, his sister expressed her delight at the change in her little daughter.

"Yes," he said, "Nell did not seem to have any idea that there was anything more to the song than to sing the words and tune correctly; and, after all, when you realize how some teachers are satisfied when a song is sung correctly, as if they were hearing an arithmetic lesson, and do not insist on beauty of tone and articulation, how could one expect anything else? In fact," he continued, "what one hears in recitals, concerts, and even in church, especially music of the quartet-choir type, is largely the outcome of a desire to do something clever, like your little daughter. Only in these cases the singers are thinking so much of tone quality and so-called artistic rendering that the real meaning for which the song should be sung is lost quite as completely as in your daughter's singing. How

otherwise could good singers so utterly disregard what they are singing about? Such
singers remind one of the story of the steamer
on the Wabash that had so big a whistle for
its size that every time it tooted, its propeller
would stop. They get so busy with tone production that the ideas for which the production
is supposed to be made stop flowing, and we hear
only the toot. Strange to say, our audiences
have so adjusted themselves to this condition,
that they seem to consider that the more un-
affected by language the toots can be, the more
artistic the music is.

"But while the effect of a song is realized
through the beauty of its rendering, we cannot make the rendition an end in itself. A
song's musical beauty must be realized as a
part of the song's meaning, for this after all
is the basis of all beauty of expression.

"This brings up the question of the speaking voice. Attention to it would be a great
help in singing. In fact, singing and speaking should reinforce each other, yet the speaking voice is neglected. How particular mothers
are not to have the child join the family circle
with unkempt face and hands, and yet how
rarely one hears a mother chide a child for
indulging in an unkempt voice! We are careful to develop ideals of ladies and gentlemen

among our little people, as far as clothes and cleanliness go, and yet we are careless of that which is the most striking indication of refinement, — a well modulated voice. While it is true that some are born with a better vocal endowment than others, such variation is not any greater than other inequalities among individuals. Yet we demand that all attain certain standards in manners and dress. Why is it that with such punctilious pains for the details of conduct and appearance, the training of the most fundamental organ of social life is utterly neglected?"

His sister smiled a little ruefully and exclaimed, "Now you are off on one of your tirades about the voice!"

He laughed, and went on, "The difficulty is that we are in a vicious circle. Our vocal habits are formed when we are learning our mother tongue, before we go to school. Not only are we subject to the bad examples of our elders, but to the accidents of colds, catarrhal conditions, enlarged tonsils, strain and excitement when in a sensitive condition, all tending to form habits of vocal utterance both in singing and speaking that become second nature, and we grow up and pass our bad habits on to the next generation. It is impossible for an individual to escape the influence of the

bad example of his early childhood. Still,"
with a kindly look at his sister, "if mothers
and fathers could have voice ideals, similar
to those thay have with reference to well-
manicured hands, it would not be many generations before we should be just as much dis-
gusted at neglected voices, as we are at neglected hands. So that it all comes to a question of ideals."

"That is well enough for you," said his
sister, "but what is the practical thing that I
must do for Nell?"

"Find out whether the physical conditions
are as good as they can be," said Uncle Phil,
"even if you have to call in a doctor; and then
insist that what is said in the home should
not only be spoken plainly, but spoken so that
there will be pleasure in what is heard, in the
same way that you insist that the appearance
shall please. You know well enough that
tidiness does not come by the grace of God,
but by attention and persistent thought."

"It is easy to say this," replied his sister,
"but difficult to carry it out in the hurry and
excitement of ordinary home life."

Yet she realized that there was truth in what
had been said. She remembered how in the
circle of her own friends she enjoyed meeting those who had refined voices. She also

noticed that her mental attitude towards refined voices differed from her attitude towards refined manners. The latter she looked upon as being the result of breeding, while the refined voice seemed a part of the personality, above or beyond individual responsibility. She remembered a kindly woman whose voice was hard and raspy; while she knew a polished woman of society, whose motives she almost always mistrusted, in spite of the fact that it was a pleasure to hear her voice. Her brother's conversation made her believe that after all the voice might be found more subject to cultivation than she had thought.

If her brother's argument was true, there was, besides bad example, a wide possibility of bad vocal habits being formed through unhealthy physical and accidental causes, which might be helped by taking thought. She resolved to do all that she could to aid her daughter.

She decided that one of the most important things to do was to visit the school and see whether the speaking voice of her daughter's teacher was good. Here was the person above all others whom Nell looked up to as the embodiment of wisdom and ability. The child was in what the psychologist would call a susceptible condition towards the teacher. If the

I

teacher's manner of speech and quality of tone should prove to be refined, she felt that more than half the battle would have been won for good vocal habits.

The next morning she went to the school. The magnitude of the teacher's problem began to dawn upon her as she stood looking into the faces of forty little children instead of the face of her one little girl. How was this one teacher to look after the different needs of so many? If she could keep the children busy doing a little formal work she certainly would be doing well. And yet, she must not only do this but keep up the endless reports and all the red tape of an educational system. Would it not be perfectly natural, as the little people felt the confinement of their classes and the restraint of their seats and began to get uneasy, for her voice to become harsh and nervous? Yet it was in the golden hours spent with this one teacher that these forty little people were to get not only knowledge of reading and half a dozen other subjects, but also a manner of behavior and speech.

She had come to the school to-day in the hope that some attention would be paid to these aspects of training. Instead she discovered the nervous strain under which the teacher was required to work, and she felt that much of the matter-of-fact and unpoetic voice quality of her child was due largely to the unfavorable conditions under which her school work was done. Very exceptional teachers might do better, but very exceptional people are not attracted by teachers' salaries. Only once in a while some lover of children combines both ability and fine voice.

She returned to her home with a firmer resolve than ever to pay attention to vocal habits, and especially to the speaking voice. For this, she had found, could not well be separated from the work and attention necessary for the singing voice; in fact, as she stated to herself, the controlling motive in both aspects of the voice is the same: to make what we do more beautiful — to please. This was the fundamental problem of her brother's teaching. She realized also that love of beauty grows out of that social need upon which are based both forms of language, speaking and singing; and that this social aim should always be kept in view as the true end of voice work in school. She planned that at the woman's club the questions of training, preparation, and salary of teachers, with the number of pupils that they should be obliged to instruct, should be brought up for discussion.

Section 3

That afternoon Nell went to her uncle for her lesson.

"Well," said her uncle, "what are we going to learn to-day?   Do you remember?"

"How to make the voice beautiful," said Nell promptly.

"And what do we mean by having the voice beautiful?"

After a little hesitation she replied, "So we shall want to hear it."

"I am going to sing some tones in two ways. Tell me which you think is the more beautiful, which way you want to hear them."

Her uncle then sang the scale softly, vocalizing it with the syllables, beginning with the upper tone and singing down.

"Now compare that with the way I am going to sing it to you this time."

Then he sang the same syllables, in the same direction, but changed the quality of the voice with each change of syllable.

"That sounds funny," said Nell.

"What do you mean?   What difference was there between the two ways in which I sang?"

"The first was smooth and all alike, but the second was all different."

"Rather patchy, wasn't it?   If you were

making a new dress for your doll, would you want to have it patched all over, helter skelter, with color? The first time I took great pains to sing one kind of tone, although I took care to pronounce all the words correctly, while the second time I changed the quality of the tone with each syllable, and you didn't like it, did you? Now I want you to sing the scale downwards, the same way that I did first."

Uncle Phil gave his little pupil upper E of the treble clef and got a clear, flute-like tone. "Now, not too loud," he cautioned, "but clearly."

After a few tones down, the voice changed to the rough chesty tone that she had been accustomed to use in school. The habit had grown on her because she was one of the truest singers and led her room, and in order to make her voice felt, especially on the lower tones where the volume would naturally be weak, she had been in the habit of forcing her voice. "Well," said her uncle, "did you sing to me all in one kind of voice, or did you change?"

It was the first time that she had ever tried to think of quality in a scale, and she realized as never before how decidedly her voice changed as she came down.

"Let's try it again," said her uncle, "and you listen to the sweet, clear tone that you start with and see if you can make all the rest sound like that. And be particularly careful to sing more softly as you sing lower."

"That was better," said Uncle Phil. "Let us try it again, and instead of singing the syllable names that you are used to in school, let us sing *loo* for each tone. That was easier, was it not? But when we sing a song we cannot sing *loo* all the time, so that we will have to learn how to sing all the different words and yet keep one quality of voice at the same time. The best way for little folks is to sing songs that they like in a way that will make people like to hear them. Try that cradle song I sang to you, 'Sleep, Baby, Sleep.' It will help to keep your tone beautiful if you think of the beautiful baby you are singing to. Play this cushion is a baby, and that you are singing so as to put it to sleep. . . . That was pretty good. I will sing the song to you once again, and this time you listen to the tones."

It was the first time that she had ever paid attention to tone quality, and she was quite impressed. The different words, while they were so distinct and clear, all sounded alike. They were like a string of beads instead of a collection of different objects. A new idea with reference to singing was now brought to her. For instance, in "Sleep, Baby, Sleep," she found that she was shutting her mouth too soon on the first word, and that she must not close her lips until she was ready to commence the next word. She found out that singing a tune was not the off-hand, easy thing that she had supposed it was, but that in order to make it beautiful she had not only to feel beautiful herself, but practice over and over and try hard to make it beautiful.

Her uncle knew that if she could have come to him at first he would hardly have needed to say anything with reference to vocalization, but simply to have focused her attention on the tone quality and pleasurable expression of the thought, and good vocal utterance would have resulted. By attention and practice in such singing, a basis of good vocal habits could have been started, but the fact that she had been singing in school and straining her voice by trying to lead her class, made him decide to give her these rather formal lessons in voice production, not so much as material for her to practice as to make her think of what she was to do when she sang a song. What he planned was to teach her to sing with constant attention to the fact that she was not just performing something when she sang, but that she was telling something so agreeably, making it so beautiful with the voice, that it would be a pleasure to hear it.

Her mother, who had been waiting for her daughter in the next room, now came in and said that she would see that Nell practiced the scales. But Uncle Phil said, "I doubt whether it would be a good plan, for while she might form good scale tones the natural tendency would be to sing the passages mechanically, because she would feel no expressive content in a scale. You know," he continued, "we have no direct conscious control of our vocal cords. Over forty little muscles and a network of nerves produce the tones we want as a reflex to our feeling, and where no bad habits have been formed the safest plan is to form an intelligent and right feeling and trust to the reflex action of the throat to produce the right tone. When bad habits have formed an interference with the natural reflex action of the throat, then we have to work carefully to remove such interference; but it takes mature intelligence to carry out such a plan. Nell has strained her voice somewhat, and the formal work that I have done to-day is to help focus her attention on the problem. Such work might be done, but only under the direction of a careful teacher."

His sister replied that she had heard the children sing the scales to vowels in school, and that the voices sounded quite sweet and pleasant.

"Yes," said her brother, "we often hear good vocal exercises in school, but they seem to be a thing apart from the song singing for which they are really intended. I have heard children sing the scale beautifully to *loo,* and then sing a song directly after it with such a rough and strident tone that you would hardly realize that the same children were singing. In a great many schools the vocal practice is limited to one or two vowels, *loo* being the general favorite. The result is that wherever this syllable comes in, especially on a sustained tone, the effect of the practice tends to make the syllable stand out with a different quality. On the whole," he continued, "I should try to get good vocal utterance by singing songs that appeal to the imagination and trust to the reflex action of the throat. There will be enough for you to do in helping your daughter to focus her attention on singing her little songs adequately, that is, as to pronunciation and expression, without bothering with formal exercises. I may try a few of them, more to awaken her thought to the technical problem involved than as practice material."

His sister remembered the many times that she had heard heedless scale practice by vocal students. Even her untrained ear could detect that they were forming as many bad habits by their exercises as good ones, and she was quite willing to acquiesce in her brother's suggestion.

Section 4

"I have so far touched on three important principles in teaching Nell to sing," continued Uncle Phil. "First, singing is not merely doing something with the voice, but doing it in such a way that we love to hear it done; in other words, doing it beautifully. That is why we love to hear singing and the reason why we sing at all.

"Second, in speaking we also use the voice, but while we are not obliged to make the speaking voice beautiful, as in music, our speech is much more effective if the tones we use are attractive. In fact, success in life very largely depends on an effective speaking voice.

"The third principle has to do with how the singing and speaking voice may be improved, especially with· children, due to the fact that our vocal apparatus is not under voluntary control. We make the desired tone almost like magic, by simply wishing it. This principle emphasizes the importance of having a worthy wish, a true ideal of tone for both singing and speaking, a desire to express ourselves beautifully, for naturally they should be improved together. Unfortunately, bad habits interfere with the natural working of this magic, and hence it becomes necessary for the voice teacher to help the throat to regain its freedom; watching in singing softly downwards that the descending tones shall have the same quality as the upper ones; seeing that the throat is not tightened; that the singing tone of each syllable is held evenly and the defining sounds quickly and distinctly made; that the breathing is natural; and above all, helping the pupil to imagine vividly what she wishes to express, so that the reflex of the singing organs may have true guidance in its complex performance."

As his sister was preparing to leave, her brother said, "Wait a minute; there is a fourth problem in music teaching that I want to talk to you about, and that is, musical intelligence. By this I mean, not merely the musical intelligence necessary for beautiful expression, but an intelligence that has to do with the form and structure of music itself; what we are able to do by means of notation.

"Music teachers might be classified into two groups that more or less blend into each other. At one extreme we have those who give their whole attention to tone and song singing, and at the other extreme we have those who pay their whole attention to the structure of music itself, claiming that if they can get the children to know music well enough to read it from notation, the other side of music can be taken care of easily. There is enough truth in both extremes to make it dangerous to follow either exclusively. Those who emphasize attention to tone first, make a strong point of the fact that little children are forming their vocal habits every day, and the earlier we can direct them into right ones, the easier will the work be and the more lasting its effects.

"Another point of importance is that it is easy to get good tone, especially with little children, as an incident in song singing, as we have already seen, when the imagination and interest of the child in what he is doing is thoroughly aroused. The work can thus be done through the memorized song, and requires no analysis or technical knowledge. On the other hand, the opposing class of teachers who emphasize sight singing are right in saying that it brings into play the power of musical analysis and thus develops ability. They insist that it is easy for young children to recognize and state the differences of pitch and duration that lie at the basis of sight-singing, and that the older and more self-conscious a person gets, the more difficult the matter of singing from notation becomes. Hence the value of such practice early.

"The plan I would suggest is somewhat of a compromise between these two extremes. Starting with song singing, and making the formation of good vocal habits the most important work, I should begin by establishing with this work the habit of paying attention to the form of what is being sung, that is, the pitch and duration of the tones, and the way they are grouped metrically. Thus we should be observing not only the quality of the tone in relation to what is being expressed, but the character of the melody as well. For instance, we should notice why one melody makes a good cradle song, and another, a good marching song; and from such general observations we should grow gradually more specific until the exact differences in pitch and duration could be effectively described.

"One cannot, however, go far with this sort of work without coming upon a serious problem: how to describe what has been observed. If the regular terms of notation are employed, we have to use words and signs the meanings of which we cannot entirely explain to young children. The machinery of notation itself is so complex that it not only interferes with the thing observed, but takes an unnecessary amount of time. On the other hand, without some way of describing what we notice, continued observation becomes impossible. I should prefer to see the ordinary sight-singing work deferred to, say, the fourth grade, but prepared for by careful and systematic observation of tone values, both as to pitch and duration, in relation to the songs sung, as just suggested, and at the same time have the notation that represents these distinctions thoroughly memorized, so that when practice in reading commences it can be done on a basis of experience as reading, and not as a process of spelling each note out.

"The observations of tone values that I have referred to should at first be expressed by action. Music is called ideal motion, hence action is naturally a simple means for communicating what we notice in music. For instance, when a child has sung, 'Ding, dong, bell, Pussy's in the well,'[1] I would let her clap the way the syllables go in the tune, and after she has thus indicated her observation, tell what she has done. In this way, the youngest pupil may be made to observe that there are

[1] Published in Mother Goose Series. Rhymes set to music by J. W. Elliot.

three distinct rates of speed at which the syllables of 'Ding, dong, bell' move — a medium, a slow, and a fast. The action need not be confined to clapping with the hand; dashes could be made on a blackboard simultaneously with the singing of the song.

"With a little aid from the teacher, the child can soon diagram duration themes of a simple melody that would make the problem easy to state. The same principle can be applied to differences in pitch. The up-and-down movement of the melody could be explained by up-and-down lifting of the hand, or with a chalk on the blackboard, such acting and diagraming always being done simultaneously with the singing of the tones. The association between the phenomena observed and the thing represented must be so close that the relationship between them cannot be lost. It is the loss of this relationship that makes the teaching of notation difficult. The child easily learns quarters and eighths and reads scale intervals, but to connect these tone symbols with what they stand for in what is sung is a decidedly difficult problem. I am quite willing to grant that children may not be able to carry on the ordinary formal reading of music as early in this way as they would if, giving up all attention to tone production and to the memorizing of musical gems, they went directly at a mechanical use of the conventional notation; but the musical result I am sure is so superior that the longer time it may take is well spent. ·

"The use of such a descriptive notation as an introduction to learning the regular notation, before taking up drill for sight singing, makes it possible always to appeal to a thought process in teaching, and not merely to memory. Not only this, but the habit of observing the structure of melodies in this way forms habits of observation, of noticing differences and of comparing effects, which will later be of decided value in musical appreciation. Such a preliminary preparation for sight singing is fully described in a book entitled 'Education through Music.'[1] If you can carry out the suggestions for the observation and making of little melodies, with a play spirit, you will be doing the very best thing to lay the foundation of good musicianship for your little daughter."

"I will try," said his sister. "It will probably help make a musician of me, if it does not of my daughter. If I understand, you laid down three principles concerning the pro-

[1] "Education through Music," by Charles H. Farnsworth. Teachers College, Columbia University, published in 1909.

duction of tone, namely, making the singing beautiful; making the speaking voice effective; and, in order to accomplish these, having a clear ideal of what we wish to express. To these you would add two more principles: first, practice for observing how the music goes as a basis for notation; and second, the use of an introductory descriptive notation for expressing these observations, enabling the teacher to utilize the imagination and thought of the pupil with reference to the real notation problem.

"Before I go, may I remind you that my big girl, Harriet, is coming soon to see you about her piano work?"

K

CHAPTER V

HOW TO LEARN TO PLAY THE PIANO

Section 1

WHEN Harriet arrived at her uncle's studio one afternoon in the next week, he began by saying: "If I remember rightly, your mother told me your teacher is very particular that you should practice systematically, first, technical exercises, then studies, then new music, then old pieces. What reason can you give for this procedure?"

The question quite surprised Harriet, for she had never thought of a reason. Her teacher had told her to do so, and that had been sufficient.

"I don't know," she replied. "Perhaps she is afraid that I will do nothing but play my pieces, the thing that I am most interested in, and not leave time enough for the other parts of the lesson."

"That's very strange," said her uncle, "for I supposed that all practice was for the purpose of being able to play pieces better."

130

"Oh, of course," she replied, "but scales and studies are to improve one's general technique."

"What would you think of the hunter who went after game," said her uncle, "and spent the first half of his day in shooting at things in general to improve his marksmanship, with the hope that some deer or luckless bird might get in the way of the bullet, and the other half of the day in hunting specifically for partridges or rabbits, or whatever he was expecting to shoot? Which part of his day's work, do you think, would be the more satisfactory?"

She laughed at the illustration, and he continued: "Scales and studies are not intended for general technique. They ought to be planned to help to play better the piece that follows them. I should say that a pupil who did not see the reason for his technical work, and how it was to help him forward in the composition he was playing, did not really know what he was about."

This struck her as a new idea, and she replied, "Then I am afraid I do not know what I am about a good deal of the time that I am practicing."

"How would you like to talk over this question of practicing?" said Uncle Phil. "After all, it is the most important thing in learning to play."

"I should like to very much," Harriet answered, for she was beginning to realize that while her teacher had insisted that she put a certain amount of time on certain kinds of practice, and had constantly cautioned her about the position of her hands, and had corrected wrong notes, the problem of how to practice had never come up between them.

"Sit down at the piano," said Uncle Phil. "I will put a new piece before you, and you may show me how you would go to work to learn it."

Turning to No. 28 of Mendelssohn's "Songs Without Words,"[1] and finding that she had not played it before, he asked her to practice it. She started out with the rather easy prelude, and played the notes accurately, but when the figure was repeated in the upper octave she had difficulty in getting her hand into position and began stumbling badly. She lost the time feeling, getting the compound movement of the meter confused, and playing the dotted quarters as if they were more than a beat long. Then, finding that they were too long in proportion to what she had been playing, she got still more confused and finally stopped.

"Well," said her uncle, "what do you do next? Go right on as if I were not in the room and you were learning the piece."

[1] See page 156.

So she went back to the beginning, this time looking at the meter signature, but not taking up any one of the single problems that had caused her trouble.   She started in with the easy opening phrase, this time somewhat more fluently, and while some of the passages that had baffled her came more easily, she stumbled in most of them in much the same way as at first.   In fact, some new mistakes crept in, so that the total amount of incorrect playing was only slightly less.   She persisted, however, and finally worked her way through the composition. Then she looked up at her uncle, evidently feeling that she was not making a very creditable exhibition.

"Now, I suppose," he said, "you would look at the clock, and if the time for practicing this piece was not up, you would go back to the beginning and play it over again, would you not? So that practicing means repeating certain actions at the piano until you can play a piece very rapidly?"

"I suppose that's it," she said.

"Have you ever stopped to think what is the use of repetition?   You know everything that is on the page, just what all the signs mean, what the figures mean, what notes you are to strike, don't you?"

"Oh," she said, "that is not enough.   You might

know all about it, but practicing means working at it so that you can play what you know."

"Very good," he said, "what is this passage of quarters and eighths on the second bar of the page? You know very well the relative proportion as to speed between these notes, do you not?"

"Certainly."

"And yet you did not play them right."

"Well," she answered, "I could not think of everything at once. Just see what my left hand had to do, and there was an alto part to be played at the same time. One can't think of so many things at once unless one has practiced it a good deal."

"You are quite right. Playing does mean doing many complex things at the same time. Good practicing means following a plan that will enable us to do these as quickly and surely as possible. You practice as if you expected to do this simply by playing the piece through from beginning to end over and over again. Was this your plan?"

"I don't think there was much plan about it," she replied.

"Yet," continued her teacher, "you were to show me how you practiced. I want to know your plan, as well as the way you carry it out."

To plan one's work was obviously so wise that she was surprised to think that she had never planned how to practice. It rather embarrassed her to know what to say about a plan, so looking up into her uncle's face, she said, "What would you do?"

"To begin with," said her uncle, "I would try to do my practicing for some definite purpose, such as a recital, or to play to friends, or as a study of the composer. This determines the choice of the piece and the way it is to be practiced."

"But I have to practice to please my teacher," she replied, "and she is very particular that I shall be correct and play it as she thinks right."

"It's well worth while to be held to a standard of correctness, but if you always play a piece to please your teacher only, when are you going to get the practice necessary so as to play to please yourself? Playing a piece is interpreting it from the player's point of view, even more than reciting a poem is. If you always depend upon your teacher's interpretation, how are you going to develop your own judgment? This is an important matter. It is my second point in practice. In determining questions of decoration, dress, and furnishing are you not constantly at a loss to know what you really prefer? You try one way and then another, in order to find out what you like, and this exercise of your judgment, educates and trains your taste. How are you going to get what are perhaps the most valuable results of music study — judgment and taste — if you never practice them?"

This idea of exercising her own judgment nearly took her breath away.

"Oh," she said, "but I am not an artist. I have to learn by trying to play like those who know. Perhaps by and by I can play my own way."

"That is very well," he said, "if in doing as those who know, you learn the reasons that govern their actions. If, on the other hand, you merely imitate them, how is your musical education more intelligent than the education of a monkey? You should not only find out the reasons for your interpretations, but also have opportunity to interpret music from your own point of view, and then develop your judgment. Would your little sister have learned to walk if she had never been allowed to try it alone?"

Practicing one's own judgment in interpreting, as well as one's fingers in performing, struck Harriet as a new idea, with a possibility of fresh interest.

Uncle Phil continued: "I appreciate that both of these important points that I have made, the purpose for which to practice, and the use of one's own judgment in practicing, are points not often thought of, yet they should control all practical work. Another point in my preliminary plan for practice is to choose the passage I intend to work on and estimate the time necessary to learn it. In this part of the plan I am really getting ready to go to work, yet not actually practicing. In order to make this estimate as to how to lay out my time, I notice the title of the piece, if there is one, to see what the composer intended, and if the piece is not too long, run it through in a sketchy way to get some notion of its difficulty. This helps me to choose the passage with which to start, and enables me to estimate the amount of time to give to it. Of course, one will often underestimate or overestimate, but gradually an estimate of what can be done will be formed.

"The reason for laying out your work in this way is like the reason for living on an allowance; you know what a difference it makes whether your father gives you a definite allowance or whether he says, 'I will pay all your necessary expenses, but be careful not to be extravagant.' In some moods such confidence works well and so does practicing without definite aims, but if we are to keep at it day after day, it is wiser to limit what we have to spend, especially the most precious thing we have, time. Having to learn a piece for a given lesson often helps, but that is an external control.   We must be our own masters if we are to reach the freedom of success.

"Thus my third point is to plan to do a given piece of work in a given period of time; then when I am through, I know what has been accomplished and what it has cost.

"In preparing for practice, then, I have these points to consider :

" 1. The purpose to be accomplished in learning the piece.

" 2. The use of my own judgment in accomplishing this purpose.

" 3. The use of my practice time for the day, the length of which will determine the choice of the passages to be learned."

Section 2

"Let us see what you would be likely to do next. In the example of practice you just gave me, you remember, repetition was about the only method you followed and this with little intelligence, for you were learning to make mistakes in some parts of the piece though you were learning correct notes in other parts. An illustration will help us understand the value of repetition. Do you remember when your little sister was a baby?"

"Of course," Harriet answered. "She was so cunning."

"Well, do you remember when she was first learning to use a spoon? The chubby little hand grasped the spoon with vigor enough to lift her weight, and do you remember the jerky kind of motion she would make?"

"Yes," she replied laughing, "she punched the spoon into the side of her face and once I thought she was going to put her eye out. She did not seem to know where her mouth was. She jabbed her face, sometimes on one side, sometimes on the other. But it was not long before she could carry the spoon straight to her mouth."

"She had just the one thing to do, and she kept at it until she did it successfully. I suspect that is more than you do. If your little sister had been content with landing the spoon at the side of her face two or three times and then stopped, don't you think she might have got into the habit, so that the next time she commenced to eat she would hit the same place?"

This preposterous situation made Harriet laugh. But she began to realize its application to her practice. She realized that many times after working at a piece for a week or more, she had many incorrect ways of playing so thoroughly established that it was only by the constant watchfulness of her teacher, and the greatest pains on her part, that she could change them. She began to realize that the advantage that her little sister had in learning to handle her spoon was that however clumsily she managed, she was never satisfied until she finally reached her mouth; while in her piano practice many mistakes were unnoticed and then played incorrectly over and over, until they were learned incorrectly.

"In practicing this piece," continued Uncle Phil, "you had many difficult things to do; therefore you did not try to do them all, but did what you could correctly, and the rest of them you did wrong. You reached a point where you had learned to play perhaps two thirds of your piece correctly, and the other third incorrectly. If you kept your practice up long enough, you learned these two thirds so well that you then had attention enough left to attend to the other third. By that time, however, the mistakes had become so well fixed that you had considerable trouble to unlearn them. Do you think that this is a wise and economical way to work?"

"No, of course not, Uncle Phil. But what is a body going to do where there are so many things to think of at the same time?"

"That is just our problem," he answered, "your implication is, that some passages have to be played wrong. Do you mean this?"

"Well," she replied, "perhaps if one tried hard enough one might play all of them right the first time, but it would take a remarkable person to do this."

"Being remarkable, then, is the only essential?"

He gave her time to think over this question, and finally suggested that it might help her if she considered the passage which had bothered her in the piece she had just been playing.

"My teacher has often suggested that I play one hand at a time," said she. "That, of course, does not give one so many things to think of at once, but it is so stupid playing that way."

"I admit it might be a tedious thing to do. Is that the only thing?"

"I might look at each passage carefully before I even tried to play it with one hand," was the reply.

"Then you will admit," her uncle said, "that the passage is made up of difficulties of various kinds, some of which could be overcome by simply observing them carefully, and others by playing them with one hand first. I would go further," he continued, "if a passage has some peculiar difficulty in it, like moving the hand over the thumb, or wide stretches between the weak fingers, I would pick out these difficult parts, and make exercises out of them so as to practice the particular kind of movement of the hand or stretch of the fingers, hundreds of times in comparatively few minutes. Can you give me any reason for doing this?"

"I suppose," said she, brightening with interest, "that making a study out of the difficult passages gives one the opportunity of doing it over so many times that one's hand learns how to play the passages, so that one does not have to think about them."

"Good," he replied. "Can you tell me now the important things to do in practicing?"

"To avoid playing wrong, because it forms bad habits," she answered quickly.

"Yes," said her uncle, "and to avoid playing in a wrong way one should take only a part of the piece, or even one hand, and drill on the difficult parts before undertaking to play the piece as a whole.

"In other words, one should be like a general conducting a campaign who attacks the strategic points first, rather than expose his men all along the line. Did you do anything of that sort when you started practicing the piece I gave you a little while ago? Did you not rather rush your ten little soldiers to the front without the slightest preparation as to the difficulties they were to meet?"

While she laughed at the illustration, the foolishness of her performance brought color to her face. What her uncle had been saying seemed such good common sense, she wondered that she had not thought of it herself. She realized that her teacher had practically told her everything that her uncle had recommended, but somehow the ideas had been conveyed to her as arbitrary commands, with perhaps the vague idea that the pupil would think out the reasons for them, not stopping to consider that such thinking is about the last thing a pupil is inclined to do.

"Will you take a pencil," continued her uncle, "and show me how you would plan to practice this piece?"

She skipped over the easy beginning and marked out the left hand part of the first figure that had troubled her.

"Why so fast?" said her uncle.

"Oh," she said, "the first few measures are easy enough."

"But I would commence before that," he said.

She looked at him in surprise. "I should commence with the signature; noting both key and meter. For instance, this is in the key of G. What does that mean? What are the other likely keys that would probably come in·as the piece progressed?"

This was a novel suggestion to her, for she had never thought of keys as being in groups.

"And so with the movement of the piece. I should try to get the swing of it into my mind right at the very beginning. These few measures and the signature give you the clew to the movement for the whole piece."

"But that will come out when you play it," she said.

"Yes," said her uncle, "but that would be like the general who sent his soldiers rushing on ahead of his plan, in order to find out what to do."

"But am I to hear the music before I commence playing?" asked Harriet.

"Certainly," he answered, "though it is rather difficult for most students to do. You can, however, form some idea of each passage before you try to play it. If you were going to read that motto on the wall, would you commence saying the words over mechanically? Would you not rather grasp the meaning of the whole first?"

"Why, of course," she said, "you could not read it smoothly unless you knew what was coming."

"How do you expect you are going to read music then?"

He let her proceed and she went on picking out and marking the things that bothered her. Just as she was passing on to the final passage, her uncle expressed surprise, remarking, " I should find it rather difficult to carry so much in my mind.

" We can reduce difficulties not merely by separating them, as, for instance, by taking one hand at a time ; but we can also reduce what we have to pay attention to by not taking too much at one time.   Why take that whole page at once?"

This seemed very reasonable, but she asked, "Then where shall we stop?"

"Where would you stop if you were trying to remember, or repeat something you had read?"

"I should break it up, according to the thought."

"Where does the first thought end in this composition?"

After some consideration she marked the end of the prelude and the beginning of the song.

"Where is the next one?"

She tried the melody over, and finally pointed out the end of the first theme.

L

"These, then, are musical paragraphs, and if you were laying out your work, you would look at it not simply with reference to the different parts you had to do all at once, but you would shorten up what you had to do by not taking too many of the parts at once, would you not?"

She began to realize that finding out what to do in practice was a much more serious matter than she had ever thought, and the foolishness of her procedure when she had started to play began to dawn on her.

"This, then, is the fourth stage of practice, — to break up what you are going to play, not only finding out what the left hand or the right hand is to do, but what the particular figures are as well; and besides this, to cut the length of the piece into short passages according to its sense, so that you will not have to think at any one time of a passage that is too long or of one that is too complex. For the sake of convenience we will give this breaking up a name. What name would you suggest as most appropriate for such a process? What do you do in chemistry when you try to find out the elements of a compound?"

"We analyze it," she replied. "Can we call this first part of practicing the process of analyzing?"

"That is a good name," he answered.

"*Analysis*, then, our fourth stage, is one of the most important steps in actual practice. If you will come again in a few days after you have thought this over, we will see whether we shall need to have another stage in which we are to treat the same passages differently. Before you go," he said, "I want to show you a little of how to practice some of these things that you will analyze. Let me give you an example. I am taking the difficult hand movement in transferring the figure from one octave to another, where the hand passed over the thumb."

He invented a little study by repeating the passage on each semitone.

"Isn't that interesting!" said Harriet. "Then you would have your study grow out of your piece that way?"

"Why not," he replied, "wouldn't it prove to be, as we have already discussed it, the most helpful thing that we could do?"

"Yes," she said, "and it would make the study twice as interesting, not only because it would be fun trying to make it up, but because it would help you in learning to play the piece."

"Now," said Uncle Phil, "I hope you will make up some studies that will help you to learn how to play this 'Song Without Words.'"

Harriet went home, feeling that the whole question of musical practice had suddenly become extremely interesting to her.

Section 3

When she came for her next lesson, her uncle inquired at once, "How did you get along with your studies?"

"I succeeded in playing over the difficult passages," she said, "and found that if I played them in different keys, taking each chromatic tone successively, it was a great help in playing that passage in the piece. But the studies themselves did not sound like anything."

"Probably not," he said, "it would take skill to make a study as attractive as a composition; but if you keep in mind what the study is for, that it is not something pleasant to play in itself, but that it is to help you as much as possible in learning to play something that is attractive, I don't see why your studies could not be considered successful. You see," he continued, "learning how to play a difficult figure or half a dozen notes is for the purpose of forming a habit of playing them, so that when the passage comes in the piece, your attention will not be taken away from the effect you wish to produce. As we said last time, it is really a case of relieving the attention from details so that you can concentrate on the more important essentials that really demand thought.

"This introduces the fifth stage of practice. If you were the mistress of a large house and had many complex social duties to look after, would you do well if you attempted at the same time to do the work which is generally done by the various servants of the house? An efficient person would plan the work for the servants and see that they did it, and would save her own time and strength not only for directing the servants but for attending to the many complex duties that are required of a hostess.

"So in playing, if the conscious attention is occupied with the mechanical details of what is being done, it cannot attend at the same time to other important problems. If you were to have a party at your home, the entire conduct of which was in your hands, you would hardly expect to come downstairs to meet your guests without previously having given hours of attention to all the details that such an entertainment demands. When the evening came you would still have much to think of. But having attended to the details, you could throw yourself with vigor and enthusiasm into making the event itself as interesting as possible. For not only would each one of your guests be different from the others, but they would all be in different moods, and your mind would have to be quick and alert to interpret every sign that revealed a situation for you to meet.

"So in playing this 'Song Without Words,' you have your servants, your two eyes, your ten fingers, your two feet, all combining to give a treat to your friends by your playing. If you, like an efficient hostess, have carefully planned out all that these willing servants are to do, and have given them proper directions and drill, you can sit down with confidence at the piano and put your whole attention on making the feast of music as agreeable as possible to your listeners. It would be very awkward if in the middle of the affair some ill-trained servant, a finger, got so confused as to what was to be done as to require your specific attention. It would be equivalent to telling your friends that you had not carefully trained your servant beforehand."

"I see, much better than I ever did before, what practice means," said Harriet. "I never knew how much was required, not only as to planning, but in having your servants trained so they can go ahead themselves."

"That is why we have the fifth important stage in practice, drill. Analysis plans the work for the servants; through drill they acquire habits of rapid and sure performance. Unfortunately, this drill is the least interesting part of practice, and so students do it with the least concentration. The result is that habits are formed slowly and poorly. If, however, we think clearly and try to see how soon the hand can take the motions without special effort on our part, testing the hand, not only by increasing the speed to more than what is required, but doing it in different keys, we soon find such drill can become as interesting as a game of golf. Each time you try the passage you concentrate your whole self and see if you can beat your last record at the very first trial. Sometimes it is well to allow yourself a definite number of repetitions to accomplish a perfect playing of the fragment and then see how near you can come to accomplishing the stunt.

"In other words, drill playing must have a motive in order to produce good results. Such a motive must necessarily be an artificial one, planned for its own specific purpose. Many pupils forget this. They expect to get from drill the same pleasure that they do in practicing for interpretation. Because of this confusion, they do not get their fingers trained to accurate habits of work, and for lack of such habits they can never interpret well. A great many teachers separate the drill work from the piece work so that the final motive for all the practicing is lost, and the pupils just practice scales and finger exercises without feeling the application of their work. It is much more rational to see first just where you need drill to prepare for the particular piece you want to play and then make up your own stunts as immediate motives for rapid and successful accomplishment. Children in play are constantly setting trials for their skill. You know with what pleasure a boy will throw stones. The object has to be hit in so many throws, or within a certain distance. Similar interest can be given to drill practice if we only go at it in the right way and put out of our heads for a time the artistic interpretation of the piece of music."

"I never thought of making drill interesting that way," said Harriet.

"You see the reason, don't you?" continued her uncle. "It is not just to give you a pleasant time while you are practicing, but to make you learn the passage better and more quickly."

"I see it now," Harriet rejoined. "It's for a practical purpose and not for amusement."

Section 4

"We are now ready for the sixth stage in practice, the one that follows analysis and drill.

This looking after details and directing servants is what the hostess does before her party.
Would you think a good hostess who has done
all this would be ready to give an effective party,
or is there still something further necessary on
her part?"

Harriet turned over in her mind the various
parties that her friends had given, and recalled
how some of them, although elaborately planned,
were more or less stupid affairs, while others,
without being as costly or as elaborate, were
what the girls called "just heavenly." She
felt that she had discovered the answer to the
question when she said, "Besides having everything planned and well arranged beforehand,
the hostess must have skill and charm to manage
all her details effectively."

"In other words," said Uncle Phil, "you
mean that even if everything took place as it
had been planned beforehand, a really successful party needs good generalship while it is
going on. Now my sixth important stage in
practice is training in good generalship. What
do you think would be the difference," he
continued, "between practice that was analytic
— preparing to get ready for work — and this
following stage, practice in good generalship?"

Again she thought over the parties she had
attended, and she felt that good generalship

was the ability to be everywhere at the same
time, to know just when to suggest changes in
the program, and to guide all the complex
things that were happening as if there was but
one simple and easy thing going on; but she
was not able to express herself.

"I think I know," she said, "but I find it
difficult to state. A good hostess, when her
party is going on, has everything going together.
She is not seated in one corner of the room
talking to one person, while things in the rest
of the house are going by sixes and sevens."

"You have the idea," he said; "the practice
of good generalship demands a treatment just
the opposite of the analytic stage. Not things
in detail but the effect as a whole is uppermost
in the hostess' mind at this stage. As we have
called the fourth stage analytic, it might help
us to think of this sixth stage as *synthetic*, a
process of controlling the many parts in relation
to the whole effect. This is just as essential as
the practice in analyzing and in discovering
what is necessary to make the details go right.

"The difficulty with a good many is that they
leave this sixth stage of practice more or less
to take care of itself, feeling, as many hostesses
do, that if they supply the entertainment and
refreshments the party will run itself. But you
will admit that while mechanically the party

might run itself, it isn't the kind of evening that gives you the keenest pleasure. A great many students spend years in practice, getting ready to play, yet if you ask them to play, they have to refuse because they have nothing ready to play. Many students fail in both aspects of good practice. They do not do the analytic work thoroughly, and they never really approach the synthetic."

"That's true enough," said Harriet, and thought of several of her friends who had been taking piano lessons for years and still could not give pleasure by their playing. "But after all, isn't good generalship, or the synthetic side of music, just a gift? Some have it and some have not. Is it anything that can be cultivated?"

"Let's make a practical experiment," said her uncle. "You remember the piece I asked you to play the other day; let me put that before you, and as we know now what the first stage in practicing is, let us see if we cannot describe what the things are that we should do with reference to good generalship, or the sixth aspect of practice."

"Oh," said she, "I should want to play it with expression."

"What does playing with expression mean?"

Harriet couldn't think of any answer that was not too general.

Edited by Theodor Kullak
Known as
MORNING SONG
Allegro con anima
FELIX MENDELSSOHN
Op. 62, No. 4
Nº 28
molto espressivo.
cresc.
dim.

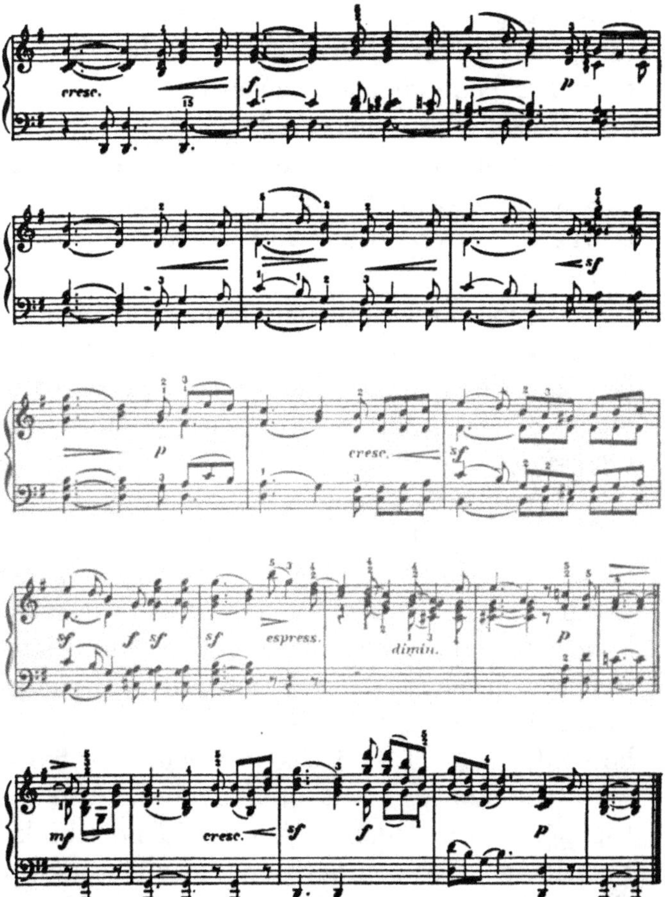
cresc.
espress.
dimin.
cresc.

"What are the parts of a song? There always is a melody, and an accompaniment. Generally before the melody commences, there is a prelude, and often after the singer has finished there is a postlude also. Does this 'Song Without Words' show such parts?"

"Yes," she replied, "here is the prelude, and this is where the song commences, and over here is where the song stops and where the postlude comes in."

"Do you find only one aspect or mood to the song, and one way of expressing the mood? Or could we say that there are two, a contrasting mood in the middle and then the first mood recurring?"

"There are two moods," she replied.

"Then wouldn't you say that one of the important things in playing with expression, in making all the details of your technique effective, is to bring out all these aspects of the composition in a way to show this relationship to the poetic mood of the song as a whole? You remember," he continued, "I said that we could not go far with the analysis without involving the synthesis; in other words, you would not think of practicing this composition clear through on the analytic basis before you gave any thought to the synthetic treatment of the same material. Rather, as fast as you discovered the details of what you wished to do you would group them into units such as phrases and periods, or parts of the composition, and as fast as such units were finished you would pass on to those that followed, constantly grouping into larger and larger units, until the whole composition expressed one whole harmonious plan.

"What would be your first grouping in this composition?"

After some thought, Harriet replied, "Why, this prelude seems to have two passages, one leading up to the other. I think, according to your plan, I should first learn this ascending one, and then learn the descending; so that instead of two passages, there would be one wave of motion up and down. Then the whole prelude will be an effective introduction to the song."

"Very good," he replied. "You could not have said that better. You would no doubt keep right on in the same way with the song, taking up first the initial strain, then the second, then the relation of these to each other, then the return to the first strain, expressing these ideas in such a way as to increase the interest; and finally you would so play the postlude that it would form a fitting close for all that preceded it. Now, don't you see how important it would be for you, when you are analyzing the composition and breaking it up into bits, to be constantly reversing your procedure and grouping these bits together into larger and larger wholes? For you need just as much practice in uniting the separate effects that go to make up these larger and larger units as you need in learning the units themselves.

"Don't you think our name for this kind of practice, that of good generalship, or synthetic practice, is a good one? Have you ever thought with what care not only the nations of Europe but our own country as well, prepare their officers to control and guide large bodies of men on land and on the wonderful floating fortresses of the sea? The success which great business establishments have gained is only partly due to their attention to detail; it is quite as much due to the fact that they are conducted by good generals of industry."

Section 5

"There is a further stage of piano study that is of great importance, namely, playing before others. It corresponds to the practice that nations try to give to their own generals, by means of sham battles and naval engagements. In spite of these attempts at practice, an officer who has been through an actual campaign has the advantage. So in music, however well a student may marshal all his forces together in the seclusion of his studio, it is quite another matter to conduct a successful production under the embarrassing conditions of an audience. So I would say, that no piece is really learnt until it has been through the last four stages : analysis, drill, synthesis, and actual performance. The reason why these four should be grouped together is because we cannot tell how really successful the first three are until they have been tested by the trial of a performance.

"There is, however, one further consideration to bear in mind. The seventh stage of the practice process ends, as we have seen, with a public performance. Such playing shows by its success or failure how effectively the previous stages have been done, and it gives practice in self-control. What would you say this further consideration might be?"

Harriet took some time thinking the matter over. It seemed to her that the last four stages covered all the points necessary in actual practice. Noticing her hesitation, her uncle asked if she remembered what he told her when she asked him how he planned his practice.

"Oh, yes," she replied, "you said you plan your practice for some definite purpose, such as learning a piece just to give some idea of it to a friend; or only to study the composer's style, or the period of the composition."

M

"In other words," said her uncle, "all pieces do not have to be worked up for public performance, but they all need testing. Some pieces are not worth the amount of time and energy that such an aim would make necessary. The first point is to determine what you want to do with the piece and then direct the stages of practice to that end. This makes it necessary to exercise one's judgment and not do things alike, but always for some definite purpose."

Uncle Phil's ideas put practice in quite a different light. Harriet had supposed that if she studied music for three or four years, somehow at the end of the time she would be able to play successfully.

"But," she actually said, "I have been playing for three or four years, and I find more difficulty in playing before people now than I did when I was asked to play my first piece."

"Exactly," said her uncle, "the test of actual use is just as important in music as in anything else. Not only pupils but teachers become impractical if they do not check up their work with the real reason for doing it. One of the bad results of this lack of checking up is that so many teachers believe they can give a technique first and teach the use of that technique afterwards. The result is that they start pupils along a fixed plan of work, although these pupils vary exceedingly in talent. It would be like building the same kind of foundation without reference to the superstructure that the different foundations were to support. I have often observed teachers, especially foreigners, under the guise of teaching thoroughly, give young ladies whose talent would not justify a superstructure much more permanent than a grape-arbor, a foundation laid out on the plans of a Woolworth Building. If a teacher saw to it that what he gave his pupils was in the highest degree justified by their natural ability, he would check up his work by actual performances, at home, before friends and classmates. By thus making every effort to have the pupil realize the relation of the practice to its fruit in actual results, a great saving instead of a waste in time and energy would result.

"I know many teachers who would be indignant if they heard what I have said to you, for they would think that I was recommending superficial work. 'What!' they would say; 'spend all your time merely playing pieces, instead of first learning your scales and arpeggios, graded studies, octave work, and the pages of Czerny, Cramer, Taussig, and the rest!' Their position seems serious and earnest, and I do not doubt that there are many talented students who have the capacity and undoubted

natural ability in music, and that they need a
foundation in technical work as solid as such
practice implies.   I am not recommending super-
ficiality, but intelligent economy, and that what
is done shall bear fruit to the extent that conditions justify.   In other words, have the technical
work done, sufficient for the use to which it is
to be put, and not practice technique as such,
without definite purpose, — especially not to
start out in technical training where there is
not sufficient talent to make use of it.

"In this lesson we have talked over the four
stages of actual practice that follow the three
preparatory ones.   I wish you would write me a
sketch of these four steps," he said, "describing
them, and giving the reasons for their exercise.
Don't forget also," he continued, "the three
stages preparatory to practice: first, for what
purpose the practice is to be done; second, how
it is to be done, the exercise of the judgment;
and third, planning a definite allotment of time
in which to learn a definite part of the piece,
so that every day's practice shall give a feeling
of progress."

Section 6

That evening Harriet's mother asked what she
had learned from her uncle in the afternoon.

"Oh," she replied, "we had such an interesting talk about practice. Mother, I have come to the conclusion that I have never really practiced."

Her mother looked up with surprise.

"A good deal of what I called practicing, I see after the talk with uncle, was what the workman would call 'soldiering' — I was just doing things to kill time and not really to accomplish anything. And the funny thing about it, Mother, is that I was all the time excusing myself for not accomplishing anything, by saying to myself that I wasn't musical and couldn't expect to do what talented students could do. I was blaming my lack of talent for my lack of success, and yet it seems to me now that instead of being lack of talent it was lack of common sense. If I had gone to work practicing the way I go to work when I am giving a party, I think my success would have made me feel quite talented.

"Uncle Phil has asked me to make a list of the seven stages in practice. Here they are. Don't you think they look businesslike? The first three are preparatory, and the last four are what you actually do when practicing.

" 1. Decide the purpose to be accomplished in learning the piece.

" 2. The use of one's own judgment.

" 3. Planning one's practice time.

"4. Analysis: when you think the whole through, divide it into its parts and choose particular difficulties to be mastered.

"5. Drill: when you practice these difficulties until they become easy — the drill, you see, growing directly out of the need of a piece.

"6. Synthesis: when you put parts together and think of the effect of the whole.

"7. Application: when you play to people and see if your practice has been successful.

"I see more and more that I have failed not only in the first three ways of practicing, but in this last way, too; for I have practiced piece after piece, and just as I was getting to play one respectably I would begin another.

"Mother," said the girl, straightening up and looking seriously into her mother's eyes, "it is very demoralizing to be always getting ready to do things and never having a chance to check yourself up. It seems to me that much of our time is spent that way in school, with the exception of a few studies like dancing and music, cooking and art. In fact, all the serious studies that count in our standing and promotion are things that we do not really get checked up on. We pass examinations enough on them, but how far they really affect us, for instance, our tastes, and the way we feel, all that would show whether these things are really worth while or not, we have no way of knowing; while all the things that we could really, practically demonstrate, are not considered by the school as studies of worth."

"Oh," replied her mother, "all your academic studies are introduced purely for cultural purposes, and we cannot measure culture the way we measure what a person would do in music or cooking."

"That may be, Mother," Harriet answered, "but I have always thought of culture as something that has to do with taste and feeling. It is not exactly doing things differently from some people, but in a more refined and thoughtful way; and the way the cultural studies are carried on in school has nothing to do with either taste or feeling. All that our teachers seem to want is that we should try and pass an examination."

Mrs. Brown felt the truth of her daughter's statement, yet she did not know how to meet it without more or less compromising the foundations of an education upon which she was insisting. This development of the pupil's judgment, making him responsible for his own education by testing it himself and proving its success or failure, was startlingly novel. She thought her brother somewhat visionary at times, and consoled herself by thinking that she stood for what was practical. She turned the subject by asking, "What practical changes are to result in your musical work from your talk with your uncle?"

"I am not only going to practice in the ways that he suggested, but I am also planning to give a little musicale, to my chum and one or two other friends, in order to test my practice. I am going to play that 'Song Without Words' by Mendelssohn, a little Mazurka by Chopin, and a Sketch by MacDowell. That is, if my courage does not give out. These are three pieces I want to be able to play well, and if I go to work at them with the idea that I am going to play them in such a way as to give pleasure, it will help me, I think, to work more carefully. I am not quite sure whether I really dare do it, for I am so afraid the girls will think I am trying to show off.

"Why is it, Mother, that we like to show our sketches, our needlework, or the result of our cooking, to our friends, but are so afraid to make music before them? You know how well Jane sketches and plays. If she showed me a sketch I wouldn't mind saying that I did not like it, and she would only laugh at me without minding it a particle; but if she should play a piece to me and I criticized it, I am sure she would never speak to me again. I should like to form a

little club among my nearest friends so that
we could play to each other, for the fun of the
music only. Do you suppose it would work?"

The mother's face was radiant with delight.
Her daughter was really on the track.

"I think your plan to play a few pieces to
your friends is a good one," said she. "You
might look up all that is interesting about the
three pieces and the men who composed them.
I think you could get the girls so interested
that they would not be thinking of how you
are playing, or that you were trying to show
off, but would really enjoy your music. What a
splendid thing it would be to be able to do this!"

Harriet was greatly encouraged by her
mother's enthusiasm, and she went upstairs to
her studies, delighted with her new plans.

Her mother drew her chair up to the fire
with a feeling of thankfulness in her heart.
She thought of Jack and of how interested he
was becoming in his music, much as he was
interested in the facts of the world about him;
how he was constantly surprising her with
observations as to pitch and rhythmic relations
of the music he had heard, much as he did with
reference to discoveries about his stamp collections, and animals, and birds, and the many
interesting things that happened on the street
and playground. True, he was saying nothing

compared to what most people think they must say in connection with music. Gush and sentimentality did not seem to occur to him in relation to it. Melodies and harmonies that he heard were interesting phenomena, stimulating his thought like any other phenomena about him. She felt sure that this was the best approach to an artistic musical life.

So with Nell, her youngest daughter, — her vain and senseless approach to music had entirely changed; she was so fond of her songs that she sang to her dolls. Music had become a part of her doll play. In fact, she had made up little refrains for her dolls in much the same .way that she made different dresses for them; while there was nothing original in them, yet they were all her own application of musical material. What pleased her mother most of all was that, when the child sang her songs to her dolls, there was a definite attempt at making them appropriately expressive to meet the situation. This affected the quality of her voice, making it at times extremely musical.

The changed attitude of Harriet toward music delighted her more than she could express. Her brother had succeeded better than her fondest wish.

When her thought turned, however, to her eldest son and to her husband, she was perplexed.

She thought of having a little musicale during the coming spring vacation while her college boy was at home, giving the opportunity to father and son to see the change that had come over the younger members of the family.

But as she thought it over, she was more and more convinced that it would not be a wise thing to do. This improved attitude towards music that the children were showing, could be compared to a young and tender plant. Any cold and sarcastic remark, any attempt at being facetious or humorous towards any musical effort, might induce self-consciousness, and undo much of what had been accomplished. She wondered how it was that not only in her own family but also among her friends, there was such a temptation, particularly for the prosaic members of the families, to become facetious at the expense of the musical effort of the others, unless the talent shown was well above the average. Even then, the attitude changed from one of patronizing humor to blind praise. As she thought over the matter in connection with her various acquaintances she could see that where a member of the family had ability at all marked, he was apt to be soon spoilt by the undue flattery and praise of relatives. On the other hand, she could think of members of these families whose musical talent was somewhat below par, who were so constantly made the object of family jokes that they never dared cultivate the little talent they had. She knew from personal conversation of such cases, where the individual longed to express herself just for her own satisfaction, but could never do anything if any member of the family were within hearing distance.

Thus through inability to find expression there often arose a rankling feeling of bitterness. What a beautiful family gathering could be arranged in her own home, if only her husband and son could join in with the same spirit as the rest!

CHAPTER VI

HOW TO LEARN TO ENJOY CLASSICAL AS WELL AS MODERN MUSIC

Section 1

AFTER the interesting lessons that our high school girl had experienced with her uncle on how to study the piano, she was more than willing to follow a suggestion made by her mother and talk with him about how she might get more out of her school music.

Her uncle's first question was, "What benefit do you expect to get out of your high school music?"

This floored her, for she had not thought of the music work as leading to any advantage. Her attitude towards the two music periods in school was like that towards recreation, and she felt justified in this position, for she knew that it was practically the attitude held, not only by the principal, but by the teachers as well.

So she replied, "I do not know if there is any advantage in the subject apart from the rest it gives from the other recitation periods."

"What would give value to your music work?" he asked her.

"If we could have a chorus of those who could sing and read music, we could improve our music reading, and learn a lot of beautiful music. I should think both of these results might be valuable."

"Yes," he answered, "the reason you do not get such results is because, unlike other subjects, pupils are put into music classes largely to fit the convenience of the school program. No serious advance in knowledge or skill is planned. If there were, there would be prerequisites for such work. Instead, even the pupil's taste is not regarded. Every one is forced to go through the form of reading and singing music, when perhaps another art subject would better fit the needs of some pupils. As this is purely a question of school organization, I don't see that I can do much in the line of suggestion. Is there any other form of music work that you are doing in school?"

"We have not time in school to carry on any other," she said, "but some of us have organized a little music club and are going to meet the teacher once a week after school hours. I wish," continued she, "that you would come and talk to our club some day."

"Before talking to the others, I should like

to find out what value you expect to receive from your club."

"I think you have value on the brain," she said mischievously.

"Yes, I have; we should do fewer foolish things if we insisted on getting adequate return for the time and energy we spend. If the children in American schools felt as I do, there would be the biggest strike the world ever witnessed. The difficulty is children do not know what they want. My aim in asking you the question with reference to the value of the work to you, is to make you think of how you wish to benefit from the study, for that is the first step in getting satisfactory results."

Harriet felt her imagination stimulated. How many times she had felt rebellious, not at the work required, but at its seeming aimlessness!

"I should like to know how to enjoy fine music, so-called classical music, the kind one hears at the best concerts, as well as this very modern music. Some of my friends are so enthusiastic about such music, I sometimes think they are bluffing; and then again it seems as if they enjoy music that I cannot. I should like, anyway, to be able to judge for myself. Don't you suppose I could learn enough in this club to be able to do so?"

"I don't see why the club might not be a great help in this direction. We can then call the value you expect to receive from the club, the ability to appreciate classical music, as well as modern or new music; and the subject of your club work would be: 'How to learn to appreciate old and new music.'"

"That's it," was her pleased reply.

"It would prepare you for what I might say to your club if we could talk over the points to be considered in listening to this sort of music. The first is that it demands concentration and sympathetic mental activity on the part of the listener; second, it requires knowledge about what we are to hear. There should be three topics under this latter head: information as to the purpose and origin of the composition; acquaintance with the leading themes; and some notion of the structure or form of the composition. Finally, there is also another important point, — a willingness to trust to feeling rather than to formulas and customs.

"Now let us consider the first point, — the need for activity on our part. It is quite the custom to announce in the papers the names of the singers and players but not the pieces they are to play. And people come to hear their favorites perform with much the same interest that they go to a horse race. It is perfectly justifiable for a professional musician or a student of singing or playing to hear how a noted artist may do things; but this, after all, is not the artistic approach to music. It is the technical and professional one. There is something more important than the composition or the performance that goes on when we are truly listening to music."

Harriet looked up into her uncle's face with inquiry.

"Let me illustrate," he continued. "You are having physics in the high school, are you not? Do you remember the pretty story about how Watt, the inventor of the steam engine, when he was only a boy, observed that the escaping steam from the kettle had force enough to lift the cover? As a result of such observation, he was led to invent the steam engine that has so revolutionized the face of the earth. There must have been thousands of lads who had noticed that phenomenon before. Water must have boiled in the same way on the banks of the Nile or the Euphrates, and in the homes of ancient Greece and Rome and throughout the centuries. The important thing in the case of Watt was not that the steam was rattling the kettle cover, but the thoughts which were awakened in Watt's mind as the result, and the application of the phenomenon that Watt

N

was able to make. This is such an important point that I will give you another illustration.

"You are studying the law of gravitation, and you remember the story of Newton and the apple: how Newton's observation of the fall of that momentous apple led to the statement of the law of gravitation. Thousands of men must have seen apples fall before Newton's time. Yet the fall of this particular apple becomes important because Newton appreciated the significance of the occurrence.

"The same is true with music. We are constantly spending large sums of money to hear great performers. They are worth hearing, but the great performance is only the external phenomenon, like the rattling of the kettle cover and the falling of the apple. It can only become momentous and great to you in the degree in which you are able to appreciate what you hear."

"We are going to get a talking machine and a player-piano in connection with our club," said his niece, "and we expect to listen to a lot of music."

"That's quite right," said her uncle, "but remember my illustration. Just hearing music won't make you appreciate it any more than seeing kettles boil or apples fall would lead to the great discoveries of Watt and Newton."

"I don't see how your illustration helps us very much," said Harriet. "Watt and Newton were remarkable men. They made a simple thing that they observed lead to great results, and so a great musician might get a very different effect from the music he heard than an unmusical person would. What your illustration seems to say is that we should be musical in order to get much out of music." And with an arch look at her uncle, she added, "It doesn't seem to me that that is helping very much."

"You are right," he answered; "but let us observe these two illustrations a little closer. Suppose that Watt, while seated comfortably before the fire and watching the kettle boil, had done what most young men would be inclined to do, — dreamed of some excitement in relation to a fishing or hunting expedition; some problem; or most likely of all, pictured in the rising steam a form and face more attractive than the bubbling of the steam. Would he have discovered the steam engine? Imagine Newton lying on the grass looking up into the apple tree; how many young men under the same conditions would have gone to the bother of carrying out the strenuous thought started by the accidental fall? The reason why I have made self-activity in relation to music so prominent in my illustration, is that so many listen to music in a passive kind of way and are surprised that they are not moved.

"While granting all you say of the remarkable equipment of both these men and their natural endowment, you must admit that there was at work a purposeful will, an activity, an interest, and an attention to what was going on around them. Every one is capable of doing this in some degree, according as his gifts are great or small. So any listener to music, apart from all extraordinary gifts, with only the simple capacity of attention to what he is hearing, is capable of interpreting what he hears. This, then, is our first point in listening, especially to classical or to new music; we must meet the composer and performers, at least half way, by being ready to pay the closest attention. This, however, is not different from what you would do in listening to any good music, or, for that matter, to a Shakespeare play. You appreciate at once that it demands a kind of attention different from that given to a vaudeville performance. People are somewhat aware of the different kinds of attention demanded by different kinds of literature, but not so much so in music; partly because classical and modern music demand an acquaintance to be enjoyed, — an acquaintance that many have not had. This brings me to my second point, — intelligent listening."

"I have been to concerts," said Harriet, "where I have heard a piece that I am sure was a great work performed by a great artist, and I have tried my best to understand it, but have only been bewildered and bored."

"True," said her uncle, "that is quite possible. It is a simple matter to see an apple fall or watch a kettle boil; the second remarkable thing about these illustrations is the extent to which past knowledge was utilized in their connection. Listening to a classical composition is a complex problem, one might have a serious and determined desire to make the most of a hearing, and yet not be able to get anything out of it.

"Besides a determined desire to understand and make the most of what we hear, we must have some knowledge and experience that will make such desire effective. While music is one of the most universal of arts, the various forms that it takes are dependent on the civilization that produces them. Our music is the same as that of the European, while the music of the Hindus and the Chinese, though quite as complex and beautifully developed as ours, appears almost incomprehensible to us. I have been in a Chinese theater and listened to music with a most intense desire to understand it, and have received more pain than pleasure from the effort, simply because I did not know that particular form and manner of music. In order to understand such music we require far more than good attention and the desire to understand what we hear. It is such knowledge that the study of appreciation should help you to gain.

"This, then, is our second point, that of intelligence, with its three important topics. In connection with these, serious study can be of help if it is rightly done. It is on these topics that I should like to speak before your high school music club."

"Very well," said Harriet, "I will arrange with the teacher and have you invited to speak to our club on the subject of 'How to learn to enjoy classical music.'"

Section 2

The news of the invitation spread rapidly in school, and the next day, during recess, a number of the club members talked over the novel exercise that they were to enjoy on Friday afternoon.

"What is appreciation, anyway?" asked a rather athletic girl.

"I know," said the mischievous little mimic of the party, "appreciation is having somebody sit at the piano and tell how lovely you feel when hearing music.''

When Friday afternoon came, about thirty expectant girls gathered to listen to the talk on appreciation. They were accustomed to have their teacher talk to them. In fact, the more the teacher talked, and the fewer questions he asked, the better they liked it. And this afternoon they expected somebody not only to talk to them, but to sing and play as well, and their eager minds were full of all sorts of anticipations. The speaker looked at the demure group while the teacher made the introductory remarks. He did not realize how minutely he was being inspected. ˙ Everything, from his shoes to the way his hair was parted, was assiduously taken in. Perhaps the most important of the various imaginings which were floating through their minds was the wonder why so good looking a man had not married. Was there a tragic story back of it all? Some foreign beauty, to whose marriage her parents would not give consent? Meanwhile he, with the characteristic stupidity of a man lecturing to girls, interpreted their serious and dignified external appearance as the significant interest of his audience in what he was to say. Fortunate for him that it was so, for if he had known all that was going on in their lively minds, even his rather unusual absorption in his subject might not have been sufficient to save him from embarrassment.

He played a prelude to get the action of the piano, and then paused and looked at his audience. He was somewhat in doubt whether to give them a little introductory talk, or to commence playing at once. His musical instinct directed the happy choice, and he started playing the first part of Schubert's "Unfinished Symphony." The melodies that make up the substance of this work had their effect. Even the athletic star of the class was attracted and held. Stopping after a while, he asked if any of them had heard this before. A few thought they had but were not positive, but thought they might have heard something else like it.

"The Symphony Orchestra, which comes here next week, is to play this piece as the most important number of their program. In talking with my niece, I find that one of the benefits that she wishes to receive from this club is to be able to appreciate classical music, as it is commonly called. I presume this is true of the rest of you. How would you like to have me take this symphony as an example and show how we may learn to enjoy classical music? If we enjoy, we appreciate; the advantage of my title is that it includes the feeling of pleasure without which beauty is not appreciated.

"There are two fundamental points in learning to enjoy good music; the first depends upon what the listener does; and the second, upon what he knows. I wonder if you can tell me what I mean by what we do in connection with what we hear?" he said, turning to his niece Harriet. "While you are sitting there listening to the music, are you doing anything? Aren't you just enjoying it in much the same way you would if you were smelling a flower?"

"Why, yes," she said, and then remembering their conversation, she went on: "but if I smell a rose and it makes memories come back to me of all the lovely times I have had with roses; of pleasant dinners, of beautiful dresses, and jolly dances; then I should be having not only a pleasure from the odor of the rose, but a great deal of pleasure which would come through my memory of past experience. Though I seem to be doing nothing while smelling a rose, my mind is really doing a great deal."

"That was a fine illustration," he said. "Your answer would imply that we might enjoy just the physical sensation of the sweet odor of the rose and be so mentally tired and indolent that we would experience nothing but just the sensation itself, or that we might be mentally active and have memory, imagination, and sympathy adding greatly to our pleasure.

Haven't you all received flowers, even costly and expensive ones, which have given you less pleasure than some modest violet or forget-me-not has given to you under other circumstances?"

The lecturer smiled a little, as his keen eye saw that there was considerable mental running to cover in his audience.

"You will admit, then, that the enjoyment of the flower is not entirely dependent on the flower, but also upon what goes on within you as a consequence of your own mental activity. The same is true with music. In hearing fine music the listener has much to do in order to enjoy it to the fullest extent. This is our first point. The second point is in relation to our intelligence concerning what we hear. Can anyone tell me what are some of the things we want to know that we may better enjoy this symphony?"

"Would it help us," asked one of the girls, "to know something of how music is made?"

"Do you mean the instruments that play the different parts of this symphony?"

"Partly," was the reply.

"What else?"

"Why, the first subject, and the second subject."

A titter went down the room, rather to the surprise of the lecturer, and the girl sat down in some confusion. Mr. Curtis smiled also. He realized that here was somebody who had heard a typical appreciation lecture, and he was glad to have the opportunity to make his point of the right use of knowledge in relation to appreciation.

"Let us go back to the illustration of the rose," he said. "Suppose that you had a beautiful tea rose sent you when you had just been studying the effect of cultivation on flowers. As soon as you saw the rose you exclaimed, 'This is a fine illustration of a hybrid,' and began pulling it apart so as to see the extent of development over the wild progenitor with its single petals. You might be enjoying the rose while you were destroying it, mightn't you? But if, instead, you had looked into the rose and let all your knowledge of botany and the effect of cultivation come into your mind only to make you keener to notice the form, shading, and quality of the beautiful specimen before you, then you would admit that knowledge of the structure of this particular flower and all your botanical information might serve as a sort of soil, out of which your true appreciation would grow. It is possible, however, to have our knowledge change our interest from observation of beauty to observation of scientific aspects, thus coming between the music and the highest effect which it should produce in us. A great many thoughtful musicians are skeptical about appreciation courses. The student who has studied to observe the forms in a symphony, or the way the motives occur in a Wagner opera, may be so engrossed in watching these particular phenomena that the real poetic message of the opera or the symphony can never get to him. But knowledge, when it enables us to observe more keenly, can help us in our enjoyment of the beautiful.

"You have seen also by the illustration of the rose that knowledge may be wrongly used. This brings us to the aspect of intelligent listening. Can anyone state what the question should be?"

"Isn't it how shall we rightly use our knowledge in connection with what we are going to enjoy hearing?" said a girl who had understood the illustration of the rose.

"Very good," he answered.

Another girl suggested that they might study the form of the composition, — how it was made.

"That would be valuable, but would that be the most obvious thing, something that anyone with common sense would do next? Remember we are thinking of the whole field of good music, vocal as well as instrumental."

At this, a number volunteered to answer.

Turning to the athletic girl, he asked, "What do you say would be the most natural thing to do?"

She answered, "To find out all you could about the piece before you commenced with the piece itself. That makes a good title; why not call it 'information as to the purpose and origin of the composition'? This would keep one from starting in as many wrong ways as one might otherwise."

"Very well. What would this include in vocal music?"

"The text, of course," was the reply.

"We hardly need say anything about how much knowing the words of a song and especially of an opera helps in appreciating the music, and yet this most fundamental thing is often neglected. How would learning about the piece help us to understand instrumental music?"

One of the girls suggested that some instrumental pieces have poems, or a short description, at the beginning.

"Yes," he answered, "one should think over what is thus suggested, for the key to the moods of the composition is often so presented."

"Does not a title do the same?" suggested another.

"It does, of course," he said, "but what are you going to do with the large number of classical pieces that have only the key and the number of the composer's work — as *opus* so and so — to designate them?"

One bright girl suggested rather as a guess that the number might show whether it was an early or late work of the composer.

"Good," he replied; "this leads us back to a very important part of the work we do before we commence with the music itself, that is, to find out about the composer: when and where he lived; his characteristics; what were the influences of his time that affected his way of composing; questions that a musical dictionary, like Grove's, besides the many handbooks on composers and their works, would answer fully and interestingly. It is strange how little even musicians make use of such aids. Let me illustrate with this symphony how we can thus add to our interest."

Section 3

He told them the name of the piece, and sketched briefly Schubert's life, — the poor little choir boy, whose composition was only limited by his ability to procure music paper, and how later, as a school-teacher, prosaic duties interfered with the full development of his remarkable musical gift. Gradually, with his ability to make friends, and his wonderful talent, and help from student companions, he gave himself up entirely to composition. He poured out such a flood of spontaneous music that before he died, soon after he was thirty, he had composed, besides many great works, over six hundred remarkable songs, some of them the most wonderful that have ever been written. To remind them of some, Mr. Curtis played parts of "The Wanderer," "Who is Sylvia?" [1] and "The Erl King," tantalizing his audience with a desire for more of each.

Some familiarity with these through concerts and talking machines had already established associations of interest.

"Fascinating as it would be to tell you about these songs," he continued, "I am going back again to the symphony that I started with and illustrate a second aspect of intelligent listening."

He turned to the piano and played phrases from each theme of the symphony. To his question "What did I do?" they answered that he played parts of two melodies.

"What makes you think that these tones are parts of two, instead of one melody? I produced the sounds one after the other, right along. That there are two distinct ideas here

[1] These may be found in any collection of Schubert's Songs. "Who is Sylvia?" is in most high school books. Both songs may be obtained for the phonograph.

is almost too obvious to be mentioned, yet I
realize that it is quite a different matter to say
why. What is it that enables us to group a
dozen different effects into one melody?"

Up came a quick hand. "We remember
the sounds as we hear them, and those that are
alike we think of as one melody. You played
us two such groups."

"Exactly. If we did not remember we could
not compare and group what we hear, and there
would be no possibility of music, would there?"

This importance of memory in relation to
music had never occurred to the class.

"While this is true of all music, remembering what you have heard is especially important
in connection with classical music, for much
of its beauty depends on its proportions and
the relation of its parts to each other. One
who cannot retain his impressions loses much
of the interest in the music. The learning of
important parts will thus be the main activity
under this topic. We will call it ability to
remember leading themes.

"You will feel, still more, the importance
of memorizing, if I go right on to the next
topic. One of you has already suggested it;
this is about form, or how a piece of music is
put together. This also is of great importance
in listening to classical music.

"Any long instrumental composition of this type has at least two important passages or themes. People who write about composition have classified them according to the order in which such themes appear. The difficulty of studying music from such writers is that while their theories seem perfectly clear in their examples, unless one has had a great deal of experience, it is difficult to apply these theories to other compositions that one may happen to hear. Because making music is, after all, not like making furniture, every composer likes to make his tune his own way. If we think of musical compositions as we think of furniture, — for instance, a certain part of the back or a certain part of the seat and a certain part of the legs of a chair, we shall constantly have difficulty in applying our ideas to our musical experience.

"I am going to suggest to you another way of thinking of the structure of music. As music is compared to motion, constantly changing, let us think of these themes as actors who have something to tell you as beautifully and as effectively as they can. For instance, in this symphony we will call the first three themes the first actor. After coming in and saying what he has to say, he bows politely and waits for the second actor with his theme and accom-

N

panying figure.   These two are the principal characters of this movement, or part of a symphony.

"There is, however, one other character that will have to be taken into consideration.   In some compositions of this sort he rises to the importance of another actor, and in other compositions he is somewhat like the property man in a Chinese theater, who keeps appearing only at certain critical stages to help define or carry on the plot.   Theorists call these characters First Subject, Second Subject, and Coda.   Sometimes we even include connecting passages as important enough for a new character.

"In the early classic form of composition these characters were very polite and deferential to each other.   For instance, in many of the symphonies and sonatas of Mozart, the first character comes on, acts his part as gracefully as a Greek dancer, makes a polite bow, and withdraws to one side; and then there is often a few seconds of waiting so as to give importance to the entrance of the second character.   When he is through, the third character comes on, making a low bow to the first and then to the second character, and with an air of great importance prepares for the falling of the curtain, or a change of scene.

"After composers had managed their musical dramas this way for some time, they commenced to get tired of this plan and their characters begin to become more impetuous, more like people in ordinary conversation. They do not always wait for one to stop before another commences. Sometimes the first character anticipates what the second is going to say, so that when the second character starts, you cannot always tell whether what is going on is the continuation of the first subject or the beginning of the second. Sometimes the second character commences by recapitulating what the first has said. This produces also a similar difficulty when we try to separate sharply between the various actors.

"Then again, the property man may grow very important. He may repeat what the first or the second character has said, with different emphasis. Sometimes even, he seems to be showing the first or the second character how to act their parts better. Again, instead of waiting for the change of scenery or the fall of the curtain at the double bar, or the final scene of the act, he may join in a fray with the other two and they all commence to act in apparent confusion. Sometimes, even, the property man may introduce an entirely new figure into the play. After this excitement has been kept up for a while, forming a second well defined part or scene of the act, the property man may quiet his two companions. You will surmise from what you hear that a change is to take place in the program, and that the three have decided to act over their parts somewhat as they did at first, but with such changes as seem appropriate after the lively scene just ended. This repetition of the first part, after the middle part just described, forms what we might call the third scene of an act.

"In this 'Unfinished Symphony' we have two movements, as they are called, or dramas. One is called Allegro, meaning rather cheerful, and the other is called Andante, meaning calm. These terms simply describe the kind of drama that we are to hear, and we shall have three characters such as I have described in each of them. It will help us to enjoy the composition more if we understand the relations of these characters to each other. If the first one is a vigorous man, the second is likely to be a lovely woman contrasting as far as possible in appearance and action with her partner. The third character, or property man, will be appropriate in spirit to the other two. His character will be defined by the general nature of what has gone on before he enters. You will remember in describing these characters, that in the older compositions, after the property man came in, the composers were accustomed to bring everything to a close and wait for the curtain to fall before the next scene. In the more modern forms no such break is allowed. The property man, after making his contribution, leads right on to the second scene, in which all three join; and this is followed by the repetition of the first scene.

"It will help you perhaps to remember these three scenes or parts of the composition, if I give you the names which theorists use. The first is called the exposition; that is, when the two characters and the property man all enter; the second, the working out or fantasia part, in which there is much more freedom of movement, and the actors seem to be developing the part; the third, the recapitulation, because it so closely resembles the first.

"Now I am going to write down on the blackboard the characteristic figures of the two actors of the first part or movement of the symphony; and while I play them over a number of times, I want you to observe as closely as you can how these actors perform, — whether they move up or down, whether they whirl around or sideways, — so that when changes are introduced you will be keen to

Themes of the First Subject

Allegro moderato

notice them. But most of all, I want you to observe what these actors are trying to express in their movement. This is something that each of you will have to do for yourself, and it will take all the imagination and concentration you have, to get the meaning of what is going on."

After playing the themes through, he first asked the class to hum them, then individual volunteers to do the same. He then erased the figures from the blackboard and played them again in a different order, to see if they were recognized, after which he played them as they came in, in different ways in other parts of the movement.

The class began to realize that an appreciation lesson was not haphazard listening and comprehending, but a concentrated act of attention and memory. In fact, the necessity for remembering what was moving by them so rapidly put a tax on attention and memory that they seldom felt in the studies in which they were dealing with printed material, where, whenever their attention flagged, they could easily turn back and refresh their impressions.

Section 4

"Can anyone tell me," Mr. Curtis asked next, "why the two heads 'memorizing' and 'form' are so closely related?"

As there was some hesitation, he continued: "Which do you remember better, disconnected items, or groups of objects related to each other? For instance, how do you remember what you see on the way home? Do you remember each house and tree by itself, or related to the streets that you are passing through?"

"We remember best," someone answered, "when we can connect what we wish to remember with what we already know. We remember the various details of houses, trees, objects of interest, in relation to the way we go home."

"Good," said he; "so knowing the way a symphony is made, its general plan, is a great help in remembering and keeping clearly in mind all the beautiful details as the music travels by. You see how very important a knowledge of the plan is if we are to remember what we hear, and we have already seen how important it is to remember.

"The points we have made, the first about how to listen, the second with its three sub-heads on intelligent listening, will constitute an effective plan for learning how to enjoy classical music. But you must remember that classical music is, after all, music that was written to please people who passed away years ago. Meanwhile, later generations have followed with changing tastes and experiences, and the music created for them must necessarily be different, if music is a living art.

"Then, too, young composers who are trying to express these differences must be like explorers and experimenters. They must be ahead of those whose tastes they are expressing; that is what their talent enables them to do. By what they create, they help to discover for those who are now living the music that best fits the present. As untrained people cannot grasp at once what the talented write, this new music is often spoken of as 'music of the future,' but really it is that only until we understand it; then it becomes music of the present. In other words, we look back to classical music and forward to the real music of the present.

"My third topic will be about this forward-looking music and has to do with the way we feel towards it. I, myself, will be unable to help you, for from my very intimacy with it, the older music has become such an expression of my ideals, that for me to learn to enjoy this new music would be like learning a new language after one has grown old. I might be much interested after careful study, but it can hardly speak to me as it can, later, to you.

For you, it is very important that your feeling for the new music shall not be prejudiced by theories based on the old music. Necessarily, these theories have in them no room for the new. The understanding of this new music must come, if at all, through first feeling its form and beauty. You will thus appreciate the importance of giving the new music every opportunity for favorable effect. If the music is not genuine, this will be one of the surest ways to find it out, and if it is, you will be on the road towards enjoying it. The reason I am giving you this caution, and calling this the third important head under 'How to learn to enjoy classical as well as modern music,' is that the very success you may have in following my plan of the study of form may develop your judgments of music along these lines, and you may become so accustomed to that particular structure of music that you may be prevented from further growth.

"All the points I have given you, except the one on form, will be equally effective applied to new music. This important exception is the one that will be the most difficult to manage. Modern or new music does not reveal its plan and organization. It must be felt first, — as was the case with all the past

music when it was new, — before we can map
out its structure. By the time this is done, a
still newer music will probably be dawning
on the horizon."

This frank statement appealed strongly to
the girls. They were surprised to have one
they were looking up to as to a teacher, put
responsibility rather than command upon
them, and the admission that he would not
be able to help them because of his own inability, attracted their confidence by its very
candor. They all wanted to ask questions.
The most insistent one was, "Why should
there be such a break between the music that
looks back, or the classical music, and that
which looks forward, or modern music?"

"A very good question," he answered.
"While there is always more or less conflict
between the old and the new, the break between our old art and the art of the present
day seems much more radical. I can only
account for it in this way: never before in the
history of mankind has the race been able to
change its way of living, and with it its way
of thinking, as it has in the last few decades.
The effect of such radical changes is just beginning to show itself in the higher forms of
expression. Traditions and customs have carried us along so that we have not noticed how

different the new way was from that to which
we were accustomed. Hence the new art has
taken us by surprise, and those of us who were
the most steeped in the old art are least prepared for the new. You remember the scrip-
ture story of the children of Israel who wandered forty years in the wilderness, until the
old generation had passed away and a new
generation had developed capable of possessing
the promised land. Even Moses could not
enter, though he had led them so ably. It
took a new kind of leadership for the very
new kind of work before them. I can look
from the mountain top at the new art of the
future, but you will be the ones to enter. I
hope that this discussion may help you not
only to enjoy the art of the past better, but
also to grasp the art of the future as well."

The hearty applause that greeted the end
of the talk showed how students of high school
age are ready to respond when a genuine appeal
is made to their intelligence, and they are
treated as persons who, after all, are the
most interested in the problems of their own
education. A few of them gathered around
the speaker with further questions bearing
especially on the conduct of their club.

"What is the best thing for us to do to get
the most musical value out of it?"

"Let us just run over our three main points,"
he replied, "including the three sub-topics
of the second point, and see how specifically
we can apply them." He wrote them on the
board, so that they could all be before the class
at once.

*How to Learn to Enjoy Classical as well as Modern
Music*

  I. By active sympathetic listening, associat-
       ing, imagining.
 II. By intelligent listening, requiring:
       1. Information as to the purpose and
            origin of the composition.
       2. Ability to remember leading themes.
       3. Knowledge of structure or form.
III. By a willingness to trust feeling rather
       than formula and custom.

"You see," continued Mr. Curtis, "numbers one and three are not so much matters
for study as they are for thought and action,
while the three heads under the second point
imply study. It is in relation to these that
your club can be helpful by organizing the work
and making it systematic. I would suggest
that you take the first topic under the second
point as the main study, starting, not with
the origin of music and making a chronologi-
cal sequence, but commencing with our own
music, that with which you are familiar, and

working back along the development of music. This will make your work logical, leading by gradual steps from what you know best to what you know least. This procedure will be convenient for illustration, which of course will be one of the main features of your work.

"In connection with the more important compositions taken up, you naturally would take up topics two and three, that follow under the same point. This will give you a well-rounded general plan. The next question is to work it out in detail. This must be done according to your local needs and the material and talent you can command. Don't try to do everything at once. Have a well-rounded plan, and fill it in gradually as you can."

CHAPTER VII

Section 1

THE opening of the front door without the ceremony of ringing made Mrs. Brown surmise that it might be her brother, and her face showed special pleasure and welcome as he entered the room.

"I am so glad that you have come," said she, "I can't tell you how much I am delighted with what the children are doing in their music. What is perplexing me now is to know what to do for Tom and for his father. The new interest you have awakened in the younger members of the family has not only given each one more pleasure, but a new pleasure in making music together. I am actually beginning to realize some lovely times such as we used to have in our childhood home with music, but this very nearness and common interest has tended to separate us from father and son. The trouble is," she continued, "they look on us as getting sentimental and affected, putting

207

on musical airs just to be in the musical fashion, as we put on our clothes to be well dressed. Neither of them seems able to conceive that we really like what we are doing. They look on their own tastes as normal, and everything different as more or less affected or artificial. What do you think it is possible to do under the circumstances?"

"Well," said her brother, with a laugh, "they are not æsthetic enough to choose the good from the poor music. They accept what they hear most often, and thus their taste, weak to start with, becomes cultivated for the trashy. Gradually, this type becomes their standard of judgment; hence, what is poor to you seems good to them."

"Tom comes home for his spring vacation this Friday afternoon," said Mrs. Brown. "Won't you come to dinner that evening, and let's see if we cannot get a better understanding of this matter, with a good talk?"

"Very well, I will," her brother agreed.

A few days later, Tom arrived. After considerable fun and jollity in the early part of the evening, the younger members of the family left the room and the older ones drew their chairs around the fire, giving Mrs. Brown the chance to introduce the important reason for the evening's gathering.

In a rather hesitating way, she remarked, "I wish we could have had some music this evening."

"Why can't we have it now?" said Tom. "What better opportunity could we have than when Uncle is right here?"

"Oh," said his mother, "I wanted the music as the expression of our family."

"You wanted us to listen to the kids, did you?"

"No, not so much to listen to them as to make music with them."

"Mother," said Tom, "it would have sounded like a prayer meeting, combined with the graduation exercises of a girls' boarding-school." He had in mind not only the amateurish performance, but the choice of pieces as well.

His mother smiled at the remark, but felt more than ever how far apart she was from him with reference to music.

Mr. Brown now joined in and said, "Why didn't you have the children play and sing? I should like to see what they can do."

"Yes," said his wife, "you would have looked out for their good points in playing and singing, much as you would watch for the good points of animals at a cattle show, and I don't propose to give you any such chance."

P

He had intended his remark as a friendly overture, and the turn that the reply had taken brought about a rather blank expression of wonderment. Father and son felt she was evidently much more serious than they had at first thought. Both fairly worshiped her, and were depressed with a feeling of hopeless inability to understand what she wanted, for each felt that he would have done anything to please her.

At this juncture Uncle Phil joined in.

"There are many kinds of music; we choose some because it gives an opportunity to show off the skill of the player; technique of composition and performance are the qualities admired. Many choose music for the physical sensations that rhythm and harmony awaken; their pleasure resembles the satisfaction of a cooling drink on a hot summer day. Again, others choose music because they wish to have an uplift similar to a service in a cathedral, through which their thoughts and fancies may reach out to other worlds, or enjoy for a moment a feeling of freedom and a realization that life after all is worth while.

"Obviously, not all kinds of music would suit equally well such different preferences. Those who are most interested in the performer regard the music as a means of showing off. Those who look for the physical thrill want sensuous harmony and swinging melodies, especially a sufficient rhythmic kick in the movement to stir their nerves; while the last class, looking for depth and sincerity, require an imaginative appeal in the music itself. Perhaps," he continued, "while you are talking about music, what you have in mind as music is quite as different as the two sides of the Greek shield in the famous story. Isn't it just possible that what my sister is thinking of as music and what you are thinking of, are totally different?"

"But doesn't this imply that we have a right to make our personal preferences the standard by which we choose the music we wish to hear?" asked Tom.

"We are entitled to personal preferences," answered his uncle. "At the same time we must bear in mind that the kind of music we prefer is the kind we have most frequently heard from childhood up. In other words, our individual musical experience determines our preference. In most cases, the world over, this experience is poor, and must necessarily lead to the choice of poor music. When we consider that hundreds of millions are spent every year in the satisfaction of these bad judgments, we begin to realize how important is attention to the worthy exercise of our power of selection.

"The money involved only indicates the size of the physical side of the question. Much more important is the fact that not only is the taste of those who choose gradually molded by their choice, but that the taste of the generation that is to take their place is shaped by what they are obliged to hear. Thus one hears much poor music, not because people deliberately choose what is poor, but because a very large portion of our population is unconsciously educated to like it by what they hear daily. They have had no experience capable of helping them to choose the better, and no education in music to help them select wisely."

Section 2

"What do you mean by 'selecting music'?" asked Tom; "only a very few people have much to do along that line."

"On the contrary," his uncle answered, "every time that the attraction of the music offered influences one of us to go to church, to the theater, to entertainments of any description, to hotels, or to social functions of any sort, we express a judgment favorable to the kind of music that attracts us. Our interested presence is a vote for the variety of music offered. The music produced is for the purpose of inducing us to be present because of our choice. Great pains are taken under professional guidance to please us. Those who produce this music care very little for our personal judgment as such, but they are very much interested in our selection, because it affects our presence. Thus everyone, more or less, helps not only to determine the kind of music to be given, but also the taste of those who follow us, for their choice is influenced by ours. Besides this class of people who express choice of music through attendance, there are those who express their choice by buying music rolls and disks. Think of the millions that this runs into, and worst of all, the millions of human beings whose tastes are being influenced by having to hear these selections.

"A second type of choice is exercised by a small but very influential class of people that are forced into situations where they decide by their preferences the music of the community they are in. I mean trustees, music committees, heads of institutions, principals of schools, municipal officials, and people in similar positions. While a few are well prepared to make wise decisions and have breadth of view enough to recognize their limitations, many are not."

"It seems to me, then," said Tom, "that one of the greatest questions in music is 'how to select.'"

"You are certainly right," said his uncle, "and if I am not mistaken, this is involved in the question that is interesting you as a family, for evidently you are looking on different sides of the musical shield; in other words, prizing different aspects of music, which causes a difference in judgment and choice."

"That seems obvious," said Tom.

"Before we can understand each other's position," continued his uncle, "we must make sure that we start from a basis we can agree upon as to what we mean by music."

"That is just the point," said Tom, "Mother doesn't like my music, and I don't fancy all she admires. I don't mind, however, what she likes; that is her own business, but I do object," he continued with some warmth, "to having people think that only the music that they like is worth while, and that those who don't like what they do, are vulgar or stupid. If I like a certain kind of music and it pleases me, it is worth that much to me. If somebody else likes a different kind of music, that's well enough. I can leave him alone. But I don't want him to come around and tell me that what I like is not as good for me as what he likes is for him."

"Do I understand," said his uncle, "that you mean by your statement that you deny the possibilities of any standards in music, except that of personal pleasure? For if this is so, the question of choice does not come up; everyone's choice is equally good."

The young man winced a little, for it flashed over him that his principle might be applied to literature or to any of the other arts, — to sports even, and he knew that in all these there were more or less formulated standards, which he himself recognized. While he was in thought willing to grant the possibility of standards in these various human activities, the decidedly subjective effect of music seemed to force him into an apparently illogical situation and thus to form an exception in regard to music. Not only this, but the wider outlook that college life and study awakened had helped him to throw off many of the limitations of his youth, and all standards were being questioned by him. He had met many people whom he called "musical high-brows," and was inclined rather to laugh at them for taking their art so seriously; claiming, at least to himself, that his own musical taste was as good as theirs. The tendency of this attitude was to lead him to classify these people as more or less affected and pretentious; and without recognizing it, to lower his estimate of the art.

"If I understand you," said his uncle, "your argument is that as music has so little external existence, being just a combination of sounds that are heard and then pass away, you would say the essential thing in music is the feeling which it awakens; and as long as you have a pleasurable feeling from the music, you do not see why anybody should have the right to come along and say that because his pleasurable feeling comes from some other kind of music, therefore his taste is better than yours.

"There is no doubt that among the many results that come in connection with the appreciation of the beautiful, that of pleasure in the act is the most certain; so that we can say, that unless pleasure is awakened in us, beauty has not been perceived. But," continued his uncle with great emphasis, "what you seem to imply is quite a different matter, namely: that the presence of pleasure requires us to call whatever has awakened it beautiful. This would make it necessary for us to accept as beautiful, objects that awaken pleasure in coarse and vulgar people. No; while pleasure must be present, the valuing, the worth of what

awakens it, must be determined by other con-
siderations.

"Your position is particularly interesting just
now from the fact that a group of very advanced
(and some of them able) musicians are offering
a form of music which not only does not awaken
pleasurable interest in many musical people, but
does cause positive disgust and weariness; yet
these same advanced persons are gravely telling
us that this is the ultimate and latest thing in
music, and that what the older masters have
done was more or less imperfect and faulty!
The fact that many of these new composers are
sincere, learned, and talented, makes it difficult
to account for their position as a freak of the
times, especially as the other arts — painting,
sculpture, and to some extent poetry — are
presenting a similar phase of development. If
the contention is true that there are certain
forms of music which are final and absolutely
correct, and that everything that is produced
can be judged and classified by comparison
with them, then the new compositions might
just as well be consigned to the waste-paper
basket, and their authors to some asylum for
the care of the mentally deranged.

"If, on the other hand, there is no absolute
form of beauty, and the channels through which
we realize what we call beauty are more or less

fluctuating, especially in music, both production and the forms of composition being largely
questions of convention determined by custom
and usage, much as the structure and words of
a language are, then we are forced to consider
new manifestations of art on their own merits,
and your contention that the feeling of pleasure awakened is the ultimate test is very near
being true.

"Moreover, the fact that highly civilized and
artistic people — people much more sensitive to
beauty than we are — such as the Japanese, the
Chinese, the Hindu — enjoy sincerely forms of
music so totally different from our own, points
in the same direction, showing that the genuine
æsthetic enjoyment of music may be as intense,
agreeable, and worth while to the Hindu from
his different music as to the European from
his. So your position — that we cannot take
as a criterion only the form of the music — is
justified."

Section 3

Mrs. Brown, thinking of her life work, the
training of her children's desires by making
them recognize standards in conduct, asked:
"Does it necessarily follow, however, that the
form of what we see and hear cannot determine whether it is good or bad? Are we

forced to take our feelings as the all-sufficient basis for choice?"

Her brother answered her by saying: "Let us take an example; for instance, poetry. Would you deny that a great many good and sincere people get keen pleasure from a very vapid kind of poetry often found in their hymn-books? Yet hasn't your work in literature shown you that there is a difference between poems, which can be compared to the difference between the doggerel humdrum of the plains and the crystalline beauty and majesty of the mountain peak; and that this difference is a real difference in the poetry itself and not merely in the state of the person reading it? Wouldn't a youngster just in her teens have as much emotional pleasure in some fervid piece of poetry, fresh as is the ink with which it is printed, from the pen of some 'penny-a-liner,' as she would in reading Wordsworth's sonnet, 'The World Is Too Much With Us' ?

"Or let us take another art, — decoration. Doesn't the maid, in all her cheap finery, feel as self-satisfied and happy on a Sunday morning as her refined mistress? In fact, stated by sheer pleasure, might not the accounts be decidedly in favor of the maid and the youngster in her teens? Are we for this reason obliged to say that there are no formal aspects which determine differences in taste, and that the standard of beauty must yield to the practical test of efficiency in the pleasure that it awakens?''

Tom felt that this applied especially to him and that he was in his last ditch, but still thought there was some hope for him. So he answered, ''In the arts like sculpture, painting, architecture, and even poetry, one has something tangible to make standards with, but music is practically nothing but a state of feeling and cannot be treated the same way.''

''Are you sure?'' asked Uncle Phil. ''Isn't there a difference in the playing and singing of the various college boys? Don't you designate some as being musical, and others as not? And yet this distinction is not dependent on musical dexterity or on the composition played, but on the style or way it is done. Aren't you perhaps more sensitive and critical as to standards here than you are with reference to differences, say, in the writing of poetry?''

These illustrations brought up vivid pictures of actual experiences in the young man's mind, and he could not deny that he was making all the distinction that his uncle claimed.

''I am willing to grant there are standards of performance,'' he said. ''The fact that people spend such sums of money to hear skilled players and singers shows this. The point I make, however, is this: that the pleasure which comes to us from the forms of composition is dependent on what our college professor would say was 'our environment,' and if we get pleasure from one kind of musical form and another man gets it from a different kind, the difference is not a thing to bother about."

"You are quite right," replied his uncle, "in saying that the pleasure we take in different forms of composition is largely dependent on our musical environment, and we thus happen to like one kind, or another kind, of music. We have already discussed this fully, your implication being that as long as we like it, the accident of difference is not worth considering. You grant the possibility of difference, but deny any consequences due to this difference."

This was getting the young man into close quarters, and he was still more disconcerted on looking up to see an amused expression on his father's face.

"I rather think," continued his uncle, "that while you are exercising your right of choice, based on form as well as feeling, you are denying that there can be any value in types of music unfamiliar to you. In other words, you are justifying the limitation of your musical preferences, due to your lack of experience and

knowledge of certain forms, by denying the
facts that disturb your self-complacency.

"To continue this line of thought, you have
taken what really amounts to an accidental
attitude towards music, and without any question you have unconsciously cultivated it by
using a style of music that has brought about
such a twist in your taste that you are out of
harmony with the taste of your mother. With
an assurance that would be laughable if it were
not so serious, you doubt down in your heart
whether there is any basis for your mother's
taste. You are modest enough about accepting the facts of chemistry and physics, however
they may seem to contradict your so-called
common-sense view. You feel that there are
scientific truths so well established that your
individual judgment would not stand for a
moment against the body of authority that your
professor represents. But when it comes to a
matter in the realm of beauty, you feel quite
sure of your own opinions, however they may
seem to disagree with those of established usage."

"I don't know but that you are right," said
Tom; "but you can give me credit for one
thing. I have not pretended to like what I
really did not, just to be in the fashion."

"That is the hopeful thing, not only about
your position, but also for the future of art in

our country. A large portion of our population is fairly free from cant. There is always hope for improvement under such conditions."

Tom's father, who had been listening with much interest, now joined in, saying:

"If what you say is true, we should strive for standards in art as we do for truth in science."

"Very true," replied Mr. Curtis. "But first let me formulate under three heads what we have covered so far, before taking up this question of standards. The kind of music produced most often is the kind that people like most. They express this choice by:

"1. Going to the places where such music is performed.

"2. Buying such music in disks and rolls.

"3. The musical programs arranged by officials and heads of institutions.

"The importance of making a right choice lies in the fact that our taste is the result of our musical experience, — in other words, of what we hear. If this is poor, not only will it affect our judgment, but also that of the generation that follows us, whose tastes are being formed by what they hear.

"The question of a standard by which to test our judgments becomes important, and at the same time it presents difficulties. If we choose what we like, our experience may have been poor, making it bad. If we choose what we do not like, simply because we are told it is the standard, our choice is not our own, and hence influences us but little."

"It seems to me that your last two points present a vicious circle," remarked Mr. Brown. "Our experience determines our choice, and our choice determines our experience. Isn't the improvement of one's musical taste like lifting one's self by pulling on one's boot-straps?"

Mr. Curtis smiled, for he realized that his brother-in-law felt about as helpless concerning the improvement of his musical taste as the illustration implied.

"It is not as hopeless as it seems," he answered. "Under ordinary conditions, our taste for music is as unconsciously settled by our daily experience as our use of the mother tongue, being good or bad according to the usage of the people among whom we grow up. There is, however, especially with reference to matters of taste, a very strong tendency to like what we think ought to be liked. Our minds may thus affect our feelings very strongly. You know what a change of feeling would come over you, if, when admiring a precious stone, you were told that it was an imitation. If I can tell you so clearly some of the standards

by which to judge good music that you are
willing to accept them as guides, your belief
in these standards will gradually affect your
attitude towards the music that best measures
up to them.   It is quite possible for a person
to have had a poor musical bringing up and
yet to offset this by an artistic conversion,
much as in the religious world, by being first
convinced of the beauty of the music before its
full power is felt.   Our mental attitude towards
what we admire goes a long way in producing
the feeling of admiration.   It is therefore of great
importance that we think ourselves out clearly
upon this question of musical standards."

Section 4

"Let us consider how standards are established with reference to the beautiful.   One of
the best proofs of what is really fine is whether
it lasts, that is, seems beautiful to us years
hence.   A thing of real beauty, whether it is a
picture or a tune, must be 'a joy forever.'   But
this is not all : any one individual's taste covers
only a lifetime, and the word 'ever' calls for
more than that.   The standard beautiful thing
must seem so to many generations.   Even
this is not all, for in each generation there are
only comparatively few that have the best
taste.   Our standard must seem beautiful then

Q

to the largest number of such people over the longest time."

"Can there be any such standard works?" asked Tom.

"Certainly," answered Uncle Phil; "think of the hundreds of the finest minds of the race that have for more than two thousand years admired the poetry of the Bible, of Homer, and the works of Phidias and Praxiteles."

"That's true enough," replied Tom; "you certainly do not expect us, however, to pattern the art of to-day by such ancient examples, for how, then, is art to be expressive of the times?"

"Oh," replied his uncle, "the standards I am talking about are not to be taken as examples to be imitated, for then there would be no living art works. What I am speaking about has only to do with standards by which we are to test our judgments. If we do not like what the best of the race have liked for the longest time, we are in no condition to pass judgment on the art of to-day, which, necessarily, has not yet been tried out by time. This," he continued, "is only the first of three important ways by which we can try out whether we really like beautiful things. The second has to do more with our own power of thought and analysis. It has to do with what we might call the workmanship or structure of the beautiful.

"Let me illustrate," he said, turning to Tom's father, "by the two kinds of music that your son and his mother like. For instance, we find the usual college music, the Glee Club type, employing every possible device for producing strong rhythmical excitement. The harmonies employed tend to emphasize not only the rhythm but to produce blocks of strongly opposed contrasting effects, with little feeling for significance. For illustration, in the realm of color, it is like using masses of red and green in vivid contrast to each other, demanding almost none of the discrimination that would be required were tints ˙of related values introduced. We find, with reference to the form in which these musical works are arranged, that there is the same lack of keen discrimination for subtle variations and gradations, and the same use of strong contrasts for mere stimulation. Or it is like a concoction of highly seasoned food into which such a variety of flavors is introduced that while the total physical effect is strong, the demand for discrimination is low.

"On the other hand, we find that the character of the music my sister likes is marked by a certain control and restraint. While effects of harmony and rhythm are introduced, their most striking expressions are reserved for climaxes, so that to appreciate the music, thought, discrimination, and the ability to remember are required, — factors little in evidence in the first kind of music. Is it too much to claim that these two kinds of music appeal to different planes of experience? The first, lacking discrimination, is extremely sensuous and physical. The second demands higher discriminating power, and the sensuous features are more a means of expressing some design and meaning, rather than an end in themselves.

"To sum up this head of structure: we find that it deals with the workmanship of the composition. If the standard is low in this respect, the work will be more or less slovenly in construction, as the desire of the artist who produces such a work will be to attract, produce a sensation, or to get notoriety, rather than to realize ideals in his art. He will resort to forms of trickery to get effects as easily as possible. This is bound to show in his work, even when, as sometimes happens, the artist is a consummate master of his technique. Such low standards make us feel we have been trifled with, though often it takes time to discover what the matter is.

"There are plenty of examples of what I have just said along all lines of creative activity. Take, for example, the popular literature of the day as it appears in papers, magazines, and books. How easy it is to notice the difference in the quality of poor work as compared with good examples! The sensational, poorly constructed, temporary character of one; the truth-considering, thoughtful workmanship of the other. The same distinction holds true not only in literature and the fine arts, but in the decorative arts as well. Compare the popular wall papers, print goods, furniture, with examples where a genuine feeling for beauty has been expressed, and the importance of this standard of quality by which to test our judgments is felt.

"The third head in considering a standard, entitled 'effect,' is the complement of the second we have just discussed, for it draws attention not to the work, but to the effect of the work upon us. What kind of reaction is shown by one who is influenced by it? For instance, what is the difference in the general attitude towards life and art held by Tom and his mother?

"You realize, of course, that in our practical life the indulgence in feelings of a certain type tends to develop the type. Such feelings as jealousy and hatred grow if we indulge in them. On the other hand, kindliness and the love of the good also grow by indulgence. I don't say that music of a certain type would mechanically tend to make us better, for, after all, the determining influence of the effect lies essentially in the nature of the listener. What I do urge is this, — that the kind of music one indulges in tends (more or less unconsciously to oneself) to modify the character through the quality of the reaction it calls out. The constant indulgence in frivolous music tends to develop a frivolous aspect of our natures, while the music that demands poise and self-control, requiring us to make an effort to grasp it, tends to strengthen and develop us.

"One who has continually limited himself to the sensational art of the day looks at life from a similar point of view. How often boys have been started, or been helped to start, on criminal careers by bad literature! True, the plastic arts, and especially music, are not so directly suggestive. Their coarse vulgarity, however, which is often hidden under a shimmering sensuousness, helps break up the good part of one's nature."

"Here," cried Tom, laughing, "you are making the pursuit of beauty very serious."

"I don't mean," continued his uncle, "that the expression of the lighter part of our natures has not a place in life, and therefore in art. It is a very large and important sphere of art. With the increasing tendency to overwork in modern civilization, the play side of art is particularly important. But I do object when the play of art is substituted for the whole of art, and when one's total attitude towards the subject is determined from this one aspect. The false position that necessarily follows makes it impossible for the nobler forms of art to affect us. Thus we are deprived of that which justifies even the play of art.

"This question of the effect upon us of our art standards," he continued, turning to Mr. Brown, "of the kind of interest they stimulate, — whether the excitement the work awakens is only physical, or whether it arouses our nobler selves as well, — is of importance, though it is so often overlooked. For instance, your son was not aware how the constant indulgence in light music was gradually changing his whole standard with reference to the art of music. This is exactly what happens in literature. One who reads nothing but the light and most highly seasoned productions of the day gradually loses the power of concentration that good literature demands. Such a reader is mentally weakened by such indulgence."

"I see the importance of your insistence on a standard," answered Mr. Brown. "The character of the art forms, their mode of presentation, are a part of the total influence of the art work, so that the point my son raised, that as long as his music pleased him it was all that was necessary, was not well taken. It is not only necessary for him to be pleased with music; he should also be pleased with kinds of music that the experience of the race has accepted, as seen in the standards you have suggested. It is thus that the individual makes use of the experience of the race. I realize how important this is in my own profession of law; anarchy would reign if we did not have the guiding hand of the past, and yet," he continued, "this influence may, and often does become the oppressive hand of a dead custom."

"True," Mr. Curtis replied, "custom does weigh upon us all. The trouble is that this custom is too often not an outgrowth of the best in the past. It is obvious that only exceptionally can a child in this country have that 'best' musical environment that will develop in him a union between his own musical feeling and good musical works or forms, so that the two will be like soul and body by the time he has matured. Most of us not only do not have opportunity for hearing sufficient good music in our formative years, but we are constantly exposed to the contagion of poor music; so that unless we are naturally very musical we are apt to have a twist developed in our taste."

At this point Tom joined in. "If what you say is true, what we need more than anything else for developing a musical art in this country is not so much teaching and forcing people into taking the good art by regulations, as giving the good art a chance really to reach the people.

"I see," he continued, "where my mistake was. I was right in the assertion that music, to be worth anything to us, must please us, but I was mistaken in not seeing that our musical pleasure may be perverted by hearing trivial music. I should have attempted to train my taste as I train my knowledge of the physical world, — by testing and accepting on the basis of my own observations, in the way I do with reference to the facts of the world about me. I never realized before that in matters of taste we need as much training and discipline as we do in questions of knowledge.

"If I have followed your thought correctly, you suggest that we train the judgment of the beautiful, first, by examples that have stood the test of time; second, by thought and analysis of the art work, observing its spirit and workmanship; and third, by noticing the effect on us and on others of what we admire. All three heads require practice — something to do. What we need is opportunity."

Section 5

"Exactly," said his uncle. "We might treat this question of opportunity under the two heads spoken of earlier in the evening. The first consists of individuals who make their selective influence felt by the preference they show for what they hear; and the second, of those who, by their position, are required to determine musical questions. I mean trustees, committees, officers of institutions and cities.

"Taking up the first, the selective opportunity that the hearer can exercise, one of the most important opportunities is in the home. Think what it would mean to the thousands of children who are studying music, if father, mother, and the older members of the family took pains to hear at home, and to appreciate reasonably the things they are trying so hard to learn to do; always demanding that what is played shall show an attempt to please in execution, tone quality, and expression. What stimulus it would be to such students if these relatives could show preference for those forms of music which, by their serious nature, make a greater demand on the little artist's powers! Not only would many an artistic gem be adequately produced, but the children would learn to like and value it if they saw that their elders did.

"Here is one of the most potential influences in the cultivation of good taste. Unfortunately, what little listening is done, rarely takes the art work into consideration, but by focusing the whole attention upon correctness of performance, tends to pervert the taste of the young musician. The case is similar to that of the ordinary teaching of English, which is apt to aim at correct spelling, punctuation, and good writing and to give hearty approval when these results are accomplished, even though the thought expressed be vapid. A genuine spark of imagination, real literary feeling in the work, has little influence if the petty details of execution are not as they should be. I don't mean to say that we shall encourage slovenly work, but that we shall recognize the value of the imaginative effort.

"The power of the home for musical training, however, especially with reference to taste, has been vastly extended by means of instruments for reproducing music mechanically. An effective opportunity for the cultivation of taste depends on the right selection by those who direct the home. The choice as to what these influences shall be is apparently now surrendered to the children themselves, and because of their immature tastes they are naturally captivated by the showy and sensational

music of the day.   They go to stores to get
their material and are waited upon by clerks
who never think of offering a composition, be it
ever so beautiful, that is more than six months
old.   Newness and sensationalism form their
ideals.

"Thus a stream of bad influences is being
directed into countless homes by the disregard
of those who should be responsible for the
opportunities presented to them in the selection
of what is heard.   I am limiting myself to this
question of selection in relation to the home.
The great question of music making in the
home I should like to talk about at some other
time.

"There is also the opportunity to express
one's preferences in connection with musical
productions going on in the community.   There
is hardly a town of any importance in which some
music lover does not sacrifice both his time and
money to have produced a little better music
than is ordinarily given.   It would stimulate
such attempts if, when they were made, the
members of the community would recognize
the effort by going themselves, if possible, and
by sending others, encouraging the attempt
and using their influence to make the venture a
success.   Often such attempts have failed because people who should have supported them

have not recognized the opportunity presented
to them. Indeed, they quite often discourage
these attempts by belittling what is done through
comparison of what they themselves have experienced in some great metropolis. Unfortunately, the college men of a small community
are often the worst sinners in this direction.

"I need hardly speak of the responsibility
which the hearer can exercise by an intelligent
applause of a good composition, and by with-
holding it when a work, even if given brilliantly,
is sensational and trashy. Think how it would
affect the musical art in recitals and concerts,
if people would only trust their instincts for
good and have the courage to express them!
Enthusiasm for the sensational is easily mani-
fested, and those who have the providing of
music for the public think it is what is wanted.
How are they going to know unless the honest
hearer lives up to his opportunity and expresses
his honest approval or disapproval?

"There is another very large field in which
the hearer may express himself. This is in the
church. Unfortunately, music in many churches
is looked upon as an enticing bait to attract
the unwary sinner, rather than as a part of
the worship of the community. The kind of
approval that the music most often calls forth
is an approval which is an insult to the purpose

of the worship. The exhibition of fine voices, fine technique, showy music, interjected between discourses, no doubt helps break up the monotony, and it is quite possible that devout souls can hear 'Elizabeth's Prayer' from 'Tannhäuser' given in church and still keep their religious equilibrium. But it takes moral courage to go to a church that makes some pretense in its musical offerings, and this not because the music is not good as music, but because it isn't a part of the worship. It would greatly simplify the musical question in churches if a genuinely religious preference was shown by those who hear it.

"These three classes of hearers, — in the home, in concerts and entertainments, and in the church, — comprise the great public that supports musical art.

"The second class, by their official positions, are practically selecting the music given. They, like the first class, are non-professional, yet have a great influence. We might classify them under two heads: first, governing individuals in such groups as trustees, committees, executive bodies; and second, heads of institutions, such as presidents, superintendents, principals, and head teachers.

"Individuals in the first class often seem to think that, by confessing to ignorance of music, they are absolved from responsibility; yet they allow the adoption of a policy that determines the kind of music to be given and the conditions under which it is given. One such policy is to require the music to be self-supporting, so that the financial success of the music depends upon the intake. This in turn makes it necessary for those who give the music either to procure great artists, whose names are an advertisement, or to produce music that makes a ready and immediate appeal. People in such executive positions seldom realize the injustice thus done to music. This is largely because music is mostly a running expense and not, like architecture and painting, a first charge. Think what such governing bodies might do if they were willing to encourage local organizations, both instrumental and vocal! Under such stimulus it would soon be possible to give adequate productions of works that would be a decided advantage to the community.

"Our cities are rapidly becoming centers of musical production. The controlling motive, however, in what is given is popularity. One wonders why, in a park concert, when a classic production is often more heartily applauded than the vapid two-steps that precede and follow it, the program-maker does not have the courage to offer a little more good music.

Makers of programs seem so obsessed with the idea of the frivolity of the masses as to be blind to an obvious fact. It is in such conditions that professional men like yourself can always exercise influence; and it is a pity that you ignore your opportunity, — your duty, I might say. For how shall a people be led when its leaders have abrogated their responsibility?"

"This is a new and surprising view to me," said Mr. Brown, "for I have often been on club committees, and I think I may be now on one city committee that has something to do with deciding the question of music in the parks next summer. I did not realize that I had any responsibility, except that of seeing that there was a wise proportioning of expense as compared with other needs of the city."

"Have you ever thought who finally does decide the music?" asked his brother.

"I am afraid not," said Mr. Brown; "we generally hire the most available band and let it do about as it pleases. I never thought that we had any further responsibility. But if you are right, I suppose some of us ought to go when these concerts are given, let the bandmaster know we are there, show our approval when a notable piece is given, and chide him when he is evidently playing too much to the galleries."

"Certainly," said Mr. Curtis. "Who will do this unless you do, or, unless you see that it is delegated to people of good sense who will help you in the great work of wise selection?"

"Under the second head," he continued, "there is a large class of very responsible individuals, such as presidents, principals, and others that I have mentioned, who seldom exercise the influence they might in school programs, and in providing adequately what we might call the musical laboratory of the school. Of course, we find every kind of person in such positions, from a wise or foolish despot, to a weak poltroon. Rarely, however, do such individuals adequately direct the influence that their position gives them for selecting better music. And yet what they need to do does not require technical training, only the exercise of common sense, a trust in their own feeling, and a reverence and respect for standards in music. These standards they could easily discover, if they honestly cared to, as they discover standards in literature. But I am afraid I have bored you with this long discussion."

"No," said his brother, "it has awakened me to responsibilities that I had little thought of. I see the possibility for a person without technical training, if he makes wise allowance for the three heads that you have given us

R

with reference to feeling, standards and vitality of good art, to go ahead and do something. When an opportunity comes to him, such as an official position, he can not only help the community, but improve his own taste by so doing."

"Yes," added Tom. "I am impressed with your use of the word 'selection,' for the determination that it implies will get things done which a mere attention to the improvement of one's own judgment and taste will not necessarily do."

"Yes," replied his uncle, "I have not given you directions like a cook-book recipe for telling how to select good music, but I hope I have made clear some ideas and shown the necessity for the active assertion of one's will under the term 'selection,' that will go far in making life happier, not only in the home, but in the community as well. You see I am thinking of music as a social art. I cannot conceive of it in any other way."

CHAPTER VIII

PURPOSE IN THE USE OF MUSIC

Section 1

THE use of the words "music as a social art" stimulated Mrs. Brown's thought. She felt that here perhaps was the final and ultimate thing that she was seeking in order to make music a success in her home.

"You have been a great help," she said, "in suggesting right ways for studying music as well as for its appreciation and selection. I realize the importance of what you have just said about the selection of music. You have shown us not only the responsibility for exercising our own preferences, based on what we feel, but also the responsibility for cultivating these preferences in relation to well-known standards; in other words, training for taste as we train for knowledge. It seems to me, however, that you have rather implied that when we have learned the right way, the desire to walk in it will necessarily be present and strong enough to stimulate the necessary effort.

"There is one question more I would like to ask: Is there any way in which we can strengthen the motive for making use of music? While I see that better study and appreciation of music will naturally tend to make us use it more, this result does not follow until the steps in the right direction (which you have suggested) have been made. Here's just where the rub comes. How can I induce anyone, especially my husband and son, to take the necessary steps to make the effort? They look on any attempt at the expression of the beautiful as a form of either amusement or self-indulgence, and the very seriousness with which they try to make a success of life prevents them from paying any except a frivolous attention to matters of art. I want them to feel," she continued, "that the beautiful is but another aspect of the true and the good, and worth while as a serious pursuit. How, for instance, can I make them realize that the expression of this social life of the family in music may be as important for developing the best in the life of its members as food and shelter are for their physical well-being?"

"You are right," replied her brother; "that is what we need most of all. If we Americans were as enthusiastic about living as we are about getting a living; or ever actually being

happy in our existence — the way the enjoyment of beauty makes us — as we are about
earning the physical comforts and conveniences
of life, living would seem much more worth
while to many of us." He sat silent a moment and then added:

"In thinking over history, it seems to me
that the great creative periods, when people
made the most effective use of art, were when
they were filled with some great enthusiasm
and turned to art as an aid in expressing it.
Wasn't this true of the great period of Pericles?
The national life that had blossomed as the
result of the victory over the Persians grew
vigorously, and the world has not yet ceased
wondering at the examples that it produced.

"So, with the revival of learning in Italy,
what an effective use was made of art, because
a new spirit had awakened after the long
chrysalis period of the dark ages! The community was building churches, public halls,
palaces, giving fêtes, taking such great interest
in what they did that they wanted to make it
as beautiful as they could. The result was an
art that touches one of the high-water marks
of the race.

"Again, the great Elizabethan period in
England presented a blossoming of literature
synchronous with a revival in national feel-

ing; great things were being done that demanded adequate expression. These periods
were not self-conscious about their arts. They
did not say, 'Go to, we have succeeded so well
in other matters, let us cultivate our taste by
the study of good examples and reading, attending lectures, concerts, and museums!'
Such a dilettante spirit was foreign to these
periods. Their art enthusiasm was only one
side of their general interest in life. In other
words, they had not specialized as much as we
have, separating practical things from beautiful things. It is this separation that makes
so much of our modern life ugly and uninteresting."

Mr. Brown remembered that in his college
reading in connection with these great epochs,
he had had some of the most enthusiastic moments of his student days. "I had never
thought before," he said, "how closely the
spirit that produced good art was related to
what produced great results in other lines."

"Yes," said Mr. Curtis, "though unfortunately in America the energetic spirit that has
expressed itself so strikingly in the material
growth of our country has only partially
found artistic expression in our commercial
architecture, in decorations like paintings, for
example, that have been placed in our im-

portant buildings, in our capitols, and in libraries, and also in connection with our great exhibitions. Thus, the spirit of the people has partially found the artistic side of its creative energy. Our philosophy of art is colored by our politics. It is individualistic. We still look on our art merely as a means for sensuous excitement, and in spite of the successes we have had, when art works have been created in connection with the social and community expression just referred to, we still lag far behind the artistic peoples of the old world."

"But," remarked Tom, "aren't you contradicting what our art teaches, and what those who lead in matters of taste say we should do, 'pursue art for art's sake'? Instead, aren't you making art the means for expressing the many-sided ambitions of the race?"

"I am," replied his uncle. "I don't think we can go about making beautiful things without a genuine interest in the purpose for which the thing is made, whether religious, political, or as the expression of some desire of our social life. Even an easel picture must have its message or truth. We should condemn the person in our imperfect social life who lived only to be beautiful, as we would the one who lived only to be happy. Think of the in-

fluence that such a small example of art as
'The Marseillaise' wields in national life. The
writer of this song was moved by a spirit more
than that which would come from art for art's
sake, and yet this song is a worthy work of
art.

"No," he continued, "what we need most
for the development of art in our country
is to learn how to make use of art, to connect
it with the big motives that influence our
practical life. Think how extensive and powerful is the great social feeling that is producing so many benefits for the helpless classes
of the community, and how dumb as yet this
spirit is. With a few brilliant exceptions,
we have not yet learned to sing our social feeling, to picture it, to put it into statue and
relief."

"I believe you are right," said his sister;
"you have answered my question as to how
to increase love for music, by showing how our
love for the artistic must be related to the great
motives that influence our lives. But you
have not answered the specific question, how
am I going to make my family like music
more?"

"Don't you see," replied Tom, "Uncle Phil
asks you to do what you wished to do when
you said you wanted music as an expression

of our family life. I laughed at you, you remember, and said how funny it would be; but I was only looking at it from the way it might sound and not from the spirit of having a good time together."

"Yes," replied his father, "my response to your request was also misconceived. I was thinking of music merely as a means for showing the skill the children had attained. I had evidently no notion of the social feeling, the purpose, that you were wanting to express."

"I am delighted that you see the point I have been trying to make," replied Uncle Phil. "It is growing late and I must be going. I hope, however, that we can again talk over this problem of music in your home, for it seems to me that it is in the home that the problem of the music of the country will be settled."

With this, he said good-night and left the house. Though it was late, the three who remained behind were so much interested in the practical application of what had been said, that they went on with the discussion.

Section 2

"Your brother made a good point in showing the relation of artistic activity to a living purpose," said Mr. Brown.

"Yes," replied his wife, "and the first point

for us to remember is that the social life of our home should be the stimulating cause of our musical activity. What could be better than music for making us conscious of home life?"

Tom said: "I don't know of anything that means college spirit to me more than when I hear the boys sing on the campus, especially at a football game. Somehow, this music in which everybody joins moves one more than the more artistic things that are heard in concerts, because one feels the spirit. It may not be as good art, but I don't see why it isn't on the road towards good art."

"It seems to me," said his father, "that from this point of view music, is especially appropriate as the home art. How simple singing is, and how effectively it can be done without special training! Then again, I believe that children, when very young, show talent for music in marked contrast to all other forms of artistic activity."

"Yes," replied Mrs. Brown, "think how much fine music has been written to be performed in homes! After all, isn't that what chamber music means? How absurd it is for us to take these intimate musical compositions and have them performed in great halls, and how formally we listen to them.

We hear much about 'saving the home,' and yet little is done towards using music, the most social of all arts and the one that would best bring the members of a family together. Music in the home seems to consist largely in practice for the attainment of skill by the individual. Such a motive puts the members of the family into a critical attitude towards the one practicing."

Here Tom joined in, "I have heard that in some schools the reading and story-telling for developing language, which was called 'English' when I went to school, is now done entirely with a social motive. The little reader or story-teller in the class has to come forward and use the art he is learning in a way that shall appeal to the other members of the class. These members become critics, not in a dead and formal manner as too many of our teachers are apt to be, but in a live way, demanding that what is said should be effective."

"That is the way we should conduct the music in our homes," replied his mother. "Instead of that, we make the children so self-conscious when we listen to them that they can think of nothing but to try to play without making a mistake. In fact, this was the way that my old teacher used to affect me. I remember how often when he came to the

house while I was practicing, he would sing
out, 'F sharp, little girl,' before he even entered
the room. It got so that I used to make mistakes as soon as I heard his footsteps, because
I thought of nothing but mistakes when he was
about. In fact, I think he enjoyed teaching
me partly because of the superiority that cor-
recting mistakes made him feel. I never knew
him to draw attention in any way to the fact
that I was to interpret anything by thinking
it out myself, or that I might give pleasure
with my music. To satisfy his autocratic
demands was the only idea that he inspired in
me. Fortunately, I had other influences that
made good what I lacked from him. And
yet, how many children do not have such opportunity! My F sharp teacher was very
long ago," she concluded; "the question now
is, how to get results in our own home."

"Uncle Phil has given us two good points,"
said Tom, "the need of a purpose for vitaliz-
ing music, and the value of the social life of
the home as a means for accomplishing this.
Now the third question is, How to do it. This
is a question that will require a good deal of
thinking over."

"I am afraid I must leave you to do that,"
said his mother, "and go and see if the children
are all right," and with this she said good-

night and left the men of the family, who were now so aroused on the subject, that instead of dropping the question they lit new cigars and prepared for one of those fine discussions lasting into the small hours, that both of them so enjoyed.

Section 3

After a few vigorous puffs at his cigar, Mr. Brown turned to his son:

"Your uncle makes out a pretty good case for the value he puts on the appreciation of the beautiful, whether in nature or in art. To look at the question from a social as well as an individual point of view presents a phase of the subject of which I had not thought. One may lose more than artistic enjoyment in neglecting the æsthetic. It is a fundamental principle of life that we develop power in the line of our activities. The old illustration from biology comes to me, of birds losing their power to fly because they prefer to run for their food.

"As I look over my experiences," he continued, "it seems to me as though the same law was at work in my case. I remember my interest in literature was developed by going to an enthusiastic English teacher, and I had dreams of writing plays. I think I tried

my hand at some poetry. Anyway, in my
college days I read and studied Shakespeare
with a greater interest than anything else I
ever did. I was also more or less interested
in the other arts. I used to go to the opera and
concerts when I had the chance, and I remember
a course in modern art that interested me so
much that I found myself noticing picturesque
things and stopping at picture stores and going into the galleries, whenever I had an opportunity.

"Bearing especially on the social side, I
remember after we were first married, your
mother and I had some of our best times together in the pursuit of just such things. But
that was more than twenty-five years ago,
and I think I can safely say that it is more than
a dozen years since I opened a volume of
Shakespeare. Not only did my law school
course stop short any æsthetic indulgence,
as I have always regarded it, but going in as
a junior partner of the law firm made it very
clear to me that success was dependent entirely
upon focusing every bit of my attention on
professional business. This, I now see, has
cost me not only pleasure in beauty, but also
some of the finer pleasure in family life."

Tom looked with interest into his father's
face, for he had grown to thinking of the "old

man " (as he spoke of him to the boys) as a
sort of money-making machine. In fact, he
had rather thought his father preferred making
money to doing anything else. That he should
have cared about pictures and concerts when
he did not have to, and that he had actually
read Shakespeare with enthusiasm, and tried
to write poetry, seemed so unlike him. It
put his father into such a new light that he
felt as if he were getting acquainted with a
new person. The striking contrast between
his own idea of his father and what that
father had just been saying of himself was a
direct proof of the force of the illustration as
to the tendency to lose the capacity for what
we do not utilize.

"The problem presents itself in two ways
to my mind," continued his father; "it might
have been possible for me to have done some
of the things that your uncle suggests, and
been equally successful in my profession; or
it might be that it would have been more worth
while to have been less successful in my profession, and done more of these things. If
time and vitality were taken up entirely in
one kind of pursuit it might not leave room
for anything else. On the other hand, it is
quite true that in the expenditure of nervous
energy, a certain amount of variety and change

makes it possible, with a given amount of energy, to reach a higher degree of efficiency. I must confess that from my law school days on, there have been many hours of work done at a state of reduced efficiency, due largely to such lack of variety and interest in what I was doing, and in fact induced by it. So that, busy as I was, it does not exactly follow that I could not have carried on some of these æsthetic pursuits and done not only just as good but perhaps better work in my profession.

"No doubt," he continued, "if I had done what your uncle suggests, the family as well as I would have been happier; that is, if in doing so I had not dropped much below my present success in my profession, as I think we may assume. For instance, I might have kept on going to concerts and opera with your mother, — not as I do now, very occasionally, just to please her. Knowing my attitude, she avoids asking me whenever she can. If I could go now with an actual liking for the thing, similar to hers, and realize the value of the companionship, I can imagine that her own enjoyment would be more than doubled, and my real pleasure would well repay me.

"Again, if I had kept up my interest in Shakespeare; had introduced you as a boy to Shakespeare; if we, for instance, had read together the various comedies and had had all the pleasant associations that such a companionship means, I think your enjoyment of Shakespeare would be much more extensive and vivid than it is now, and I should have had a companionship with you and an interest in dramatic art which would have added immensely to my present rather prosaic life.

"If I had spent a little time in enjoying nature and art, as Harriet does now, I should probably not feel so much the loss of her childhood, when she enjoyed nothing better than climbing up into my lap and hearing my stories. Now she is so much more interested in walks and drives with young men, in concerts, and shows of all sorts, that I have lost my companionship with her. In other words, in dropping the æsthetic, I have dropped the social life as well. I have not only reduced the enjoyment of life that was possible to all three of you, but my own enjoyment three times over. Looking at it from this point of view, I see that I have lost much more than the æsthetic pleasure."

"Then," said Tom, "your estimate of the worth of the æsthetic would be largely determined by things that were not really æsthetic, like preserving companionship?"

s

"I appreciate the point of your question," said his father, "for my statement seems to imply that I was sorry not to have attended concerts, read Shakespeare, gone to art exhibitions, because of the loss of companionship with your mother, yourself, and your sister. But as these social results would not have been possible without some true artistic appreciation on my part, I was simply implying my artistic loss, when stating the social. In fact, the purely artistic loss could only be stated in terms of lost pleasure, as there is no way of measuring this. Hence, in stating the degree of loss, while the loss of comradeship would be a controlling influence, the true æsthetic attitude would have to be present, which would be, to put it plainly, doing these things for the sake of the pleasure inherent in their beauty, without analyzing too nicely where all the pleasure comes from. Otherwise, our pursuit of the beautiful would be like being honest and decent, not because we really loved to be honest and decent and enjoyed such behavior for its own sake, but because we thought it was the best policy and produced the best social results.

"There are, for instance, two persons whom I need not name," he continued with a smile. "About one, you can't help thinking that his

punctilious observance of all religious obli-
gations is only an aspect of his canny selfish-
ness. He is not only looking out for himself
in this world, but in the world to come as well.
With the other, who seems equally punctilious,
you feel that his carrying out of all his religious
duties is done with such love and loyalty,
that they would be so done even if there were
no happy consequences in the hereafter to pay
for it. In other words, the love of the true,
the love of the beautiful, and the love of the
good, are alike in this. In order to be genuine,
the love for these qualities must be for their
own sake, must be disinterested rather than
for any practical results that may follow.

"Let me illustrate: if we are going to carry
out a successful artistic experiment such as
your uncle suggests, we shall have to plan
for an occasion connected with some worth-
while event in our family life and then have a
genuine interest in celebrating this event as
effectively as we can. That would mean as
beautifully as we can. So, while the occasion
is the reason for the beauty we seek, at the
same time the beauty is sought for its own
sake, for only through its means would our
celebration become adequate. Hence, the
greater our desire to celebrate, the greater our
desire for beauty would be. This shows the

necessity for a purpose in art besides that for the sake of good art."

Section 4

After a few moments of silence Tom said with animation, "I have thought of a good occasion. Mother is to have a birthday soon after I return from college this spring, not many weeks off. Let us plan a celebration in the form of a musicale for her." And gradually warming to the idea, as it developed in his mind, he said: "Let us get not only everyone in the family to do something, but let us have some music together."

The idea of celebrating the birthday struck Mr. Brown with considerable interest, but that he should take part in any musical performance seemed too grotesque to think of.

"Didn't you sing college songs, Father, when you were in college?"

"I did," he said; "I even tried for the Glee Club, but that was a long time ago."

"Never mind," said Tom. "I know some of those songs that you sang must still be in our books. Let us meet, and I'll select one or two songs. While I make a bluff at the air, you can manage the bass."

And then with still more enthusiasm: "Look here," he said, "you come down to the

college in a few weeks. I will get the songs
and we will find a piano where there are no
boys and try them over. Then we can have a
few four-part songs or hymns, in which you
can take the bass, I will take the tenor, and
from the way the kid is learning to read I know
he can easily carry the alto, while the two girls
can take the soprano. Won't that be fun!
Sister can have a few piano pieces and the
youngsters can sing some of their school songs."

"Aren't you going to ask your uncle to do
something?"

The boy thought for a few moments and
then said, "I don't believe I will; we don't
like to mix professionals and amateurs in
athletics. This is just going to be an amateur
musicale in honor of Mother, and I think we
would all do better if Uncle wasn't there."

Mr. Brown agreed. It certainly relieved
him of some embarrassment. Still, the proposition was so unique, he did not quite know
what attitude to take. The suggestions were
all along the line of the experiments that his
brother had suggested; they might really
test whether time and energy spent with a
conscious effort at æsthetic activities might
not be worth while, measured simply by the
happiness that they give. So he agreed that
Tom should tell the other children and that

they were to keep the affair a strict secret from their mother.

When Mr. Brown started a few weeks later to visit Tom at college, early spring was just maturing into a luscious beauty that made even the most prosaic mortal have a bacchanalian feeling. As the train pulled out, he quite lost himself in the beauty of the sights from the car windows. Ordinarily on such an occasion he would have had some professional papers with him, not to speak of the one or two newspapers, and though he would have looked up occasionally from the window and remarked what a beautiful day it was, his mind would have been steadily occupied. But after his conversation with Mr. Curtis, he deliberately determined to leave all papers behind and give himself up to the beauty of the landscape, with a perfectly clear conscience that he was carrying out the conditions of the experiment.

He soon found that he was not feeling just as usual. He recalled boyhood days on the farm when occasionally in the spring the old family horse used to be taken out and let loose on the green near the house. The memory of the coltish attempts of the old nag to express his joy by rearing and kicking brought a smile to his face, for the movements of the stiff joints had been so awkward and clumsy. As he grew conscious of pleasure in the sights of the lovely country, it made him realize that his attempts at expressing his joy, especially in the celebration, would be quite as clumsy as the capers of the old horse. Still they would be his expression, and that was the essential thing. This thought steadied him in carrying out his son's plan; he was going to be a boy again, and sing the old songs as best he could.

He had never seen Tom look happier, or welcome him with greater joy, than on this visit. The songs had been selected and they immediately went to practice. It was not so very hard after all, and in a minute or two he had forgotten his self-consciousness. In fact, he was not the old horse but the young colt, at it again, and father and son were like two chums, discussing what should be done, and making suggestions. When, finally, they stopped for lunch, the father felt that he had had one of the best times of his life already, and the boy, that he had discovered a new friend. Going home that afternoon, he had a feeling that he could not describe. Nothing that the practical man would recognize had been added to him, yet he felt a value in life which he seldom experienced.

Meanwhile, most enthusiastic work was being carried on by the younger members of the family. For the first time in her life, Harriet was realizing what concentrated practice meant, what fun it was to work with a purpose that really helped. Jack would steal away into the garret and softly sing with the syllable names the alto parts that were assigned to him. Putting his musical knowledge to such practical use made him realize as never before the worth of his attainments, and added greatly to his enthusiasm. He practiced the song that he was going to sing by himself, almost acting it out in his desire to express its spirit, and was much surprised that there was so much to attend to in singing a song. Nell was so full of enthusiasm that her mother realized something very unusual was going to happen on her birthday, and — with the intuition of mothers — that the children were going to make some music. But she had no idea of the extent of what was to occur.

The day before the birthday, a kind neighbor assisted in getting the mother away from the home in the latter part of the afternoon, so that the final arrangements for the musicale could be rehearsed. Everyone taking part was enthusiastic about the fun already experienced, though the real event had not yet taken place.

Section 5

It would be difficult to describe all that went on in the mother's mind on the birthday evening as she saw her husband and son singing the old college songs together. She seemed to be in two lives twenty-five years apart. The young man seemed so like the memory of the young man of those early days; there were moments when she could hardly realize which life she was really living. The enthusiasm and spirit of it all brought back many early associations.

But this was not all. In spite of technical crudities and lack of training, there was a relation between the performance and the thing expressed that gave to the music an artistic value (growing out of its sincerity) that is often lacking in work representing greater technical skill. The songs were sung interestingly and would have been effective even without all the accessories of association and other interests that raised their emotional effect. This was true of every number given. There was a meaning in Harriet's playing that made her pieces interesting. They were, as they seemed, new interpretations. Harriet herself was surprised and delighted at her own performance. Mrs. Brown had never heard her little Nell sing so expressively. Jack put a gusto and spirit into a sailor song that would have put to shame the over-polished performance often heard in drawing-rooms. What surprised the mother was that in this family celebration there were elements of musical interest apart from the personal relations to her of the performance. She had always thought of her family as being rather unmusical, and the double joy of the musical success of what was done and what it meant to her, was almost beyond what she could bear.

The father's pleasure was hardly less keen. He found that he was listening in an entirely new way to what his children were doing. There was an actual interest in what was done from a musical point of view, an appreciation of the imaginative and expressive efforts made that was very different from the cold watching for technical excellence of former days. He thought over the celebration in the light of the conversation of a few months ago, when he and Tom had decided to try Uncle Phil's suggestion to test his theories with reference to the value of the beautiful. He realized that on his wife's former birthdays some costly present was ordered to be sent out from a store, and that his satisfaction in the celebration was largely measured by the number of dollars he felt he could spend. What interested him now was that here was a celebration that had cost almost nothing in dollars, but it had called for something better, — thought and effort; and all this had been attended with such pleasurable results that he hardly dreamed of putting them on the debit side of the account.

The affair itself was something entirely beyond what they had ever experienced in the family. There was a family life expressed for which he had longed but had never believed could exist. Here it was, right under the surface, needing only a little attention to give him this pleasure.

Mrs. Brown's intelligent anticipation had planned for refreshments to follow the celebration. She thought that it would be very appropriate to have the music teachers and school teachers of the children, as well as her brother, join the family during refreshments. She little realized how much each of her guests was interested in what was to take place, and how substantially they were contributing to the success of the evening.

Section 6

Mr. Curtis on arriving said to them: "I judge you have tried the experiment that I suggested to you. Is it worth while?"

The grasp of his brother-in-law's hand said more than words. The conversation naturally turned on the celebration. What was done and how it was done was talked over, and uncle and teachers were keenly interested.

"I am thoroughly convinced," said Mr. Brown, "that what we need more than anything else in this hurried, worried, intensely active life that we are leading, is just this sort of occasion for expressing a side of the inner nature that is not expressed in the ordinary humdrum existence of everyday life. All the pleasure that we have had from this celebration is the result of a little thought and planning.

"You know," he said, turning to the school teachers, "it seems to me that one of the best things that schools could do would be to cultivate this spirit of celebration, — celebrations in relation to our great men, to our national events, in fact to everything that is of value, especially to the human spirit. I cannot conceive of anything that would do more for establishing in young people true appreciation of the worth of great characters than to have a celebration — a play, or a festival — in their honor. It would give the children of the school an interest, not only in looking up all the facts in connection with such persons, but in carrying out the celebration and in producing some, at least, of the forms that are to be used, — the music, acting, dialogue, or dancing. This would give pupils practice in developing and carrying out activities that exercise those powers we want most to train : fancy, imagination, will; in the ability to see how a thing is going to come out before it is done; in thinking of all the necessary incidentals that are required to make a performance successful; in carrying on a sustained effort, and finally, in bringing the whole to a conclusion.

"Don't you think such work would be much more effective towards a true education ·than merely requiring consideration of facts from books, only a few of which are ever connected with life, the rest gradually falling into oblivion? This being busy about what you don't value tends to form habits that must be overcome before life's real work begins; work for which the training of the neglected imagination and will is so essential.

"What impresses me as the result of my experience the last few months is the necessity of having a social, practical aim for our artistic activity. When we have such a purpose we seem to try in a right way to make a thing beautiful. This is a new truth to me, and has put the value of the exercise of our artistic faculties in an entirely new light."

His warmth and earnestness impressed the two grade teachers who were present, though they remembered celebrations that had taken place in school that were looked upon by all the teachers as "the last straw that broke the camel's back."

The first grade teacher replied by admitting the great value of dramatic performance in the education of little children. She spoke of the clearness and life given to a story by dramatizing it. She had realized that the thought and executive skill which the dramatization demanded was perhaps one of the most valuable disciplines they could give the children. At the same time, she described the difficulty of carrying on dramatic performances in addition to the school routine.

Mr. Curtis remarked that it was rather surprising that, after admitting the value of the work, it should be done under such difficult circumstances. "Why not substitute the more important for the less valuable work of the regular routine?" he asked.

The teacher of the upper grade replied: "You probably do not realize that the educational policy of the school is determined by the executive heads; while such heads often have had good practical experience in teaching children, it is impossible for them not to come gradually to look upon their work as a sort of big business and to introduce every change that tends to simplify and unify the product turned out. A big high school or college is like the Ford establishment for turning out automobiles; each department, or each teacher, attends to some aspect of the completed whole. It greatly helps in running such a business to eliminate all peculiarities and to emphasize all uniformities. The prosaic lesson from a book written especially to represent what the system requires, and the insistence that the pupil give a memory reproduction as free as possible from individual peculiarities, are important factors in the running of such an educational business.

"If we should now," she continued, "introduce such irregularities in the exercises as celebrations, in which the personal equation is an important factor, and the product the work of the children's initiative and imagination, you would go from the method of the Ford shop to an Oriental bazaar where some turbaned son of the South would most likely be patiently toiling at a piece of brass, or weaving, and working in with the conventional design irregularities that are partly expressions of his own fancy and judgment and partly the exigencies of his material. The Eastern product is bought by the traveler as a work of art. It has nothing efficient about it, except that it awakens love in the possessor; while the Ford machine makes the manufacturer wealthy, and the possessor happy, because of what he can do with it. The old Ford will probably gradually change into a delivery wagon on its downward descent towards the scrap heap; but the old product of the Oriental workman goes on increasing in value.

"The old fashion for school work takes the Ford as our ideal rather than the Oriental artist; for this seems like being efficient. There are, however, spots in our big country where other ideals seem to be gaining sway. As long as parents and patrons of the schools are willing to shirk all responsibility for what is being done with their children, and leave them blindly to be modeled according to the needs of an administrative machine, there will be little possibility for us teachers to change the spirit or form of our work."

"You are right," replied Mr. Curtis. "Art is individualistic, and the child that is made to think and feel for himself will be a child developed differently from everybody else. The spirit of democracy as it expresses itself in legislation and labor movements, the love of uniformity in our education, do seem to be dead against this training of the inner man."

Section 7

"Oh, what pessimism!" exclaimed Tom. "You must bear in mind that democracy has hardly found itself yet. It is not squarely on its feet. Our professor tells us that the older democracies were not truly democratic. Most of them applied democratic principles only to a selected and favored class. We have accepted every class, and we cannot develop our democratic civilization until we have worked up this soil out of which we are to grow; not, at least, until the tares of special privilege are thoroughly rooted out from among the wheat. Then we shall have a crop of grain where the average will be higher than any fruit of your Oriental or Prussian despotism, a development of special faculty and genius, such as the world has never seen."

The whole party laughed at the outburst of this college hopeful and felt that perhaps

T

after all this very optimism might be the saving grace of the country.

The piano teacher broke in here with the statement: "I realize as never before, from the way Harriet has worked over this celebration, the value of a specific motive for calling out and concentrating effort towards the development of a technique. I have always worked on the theory that we should aim to develop the training first, before attempting to give artistic expression to this training. But the more I have thought of it recently, the more I realize that there can be no point at which we can say the technique is sufficient. Every difficulty overcome clearly means climbing to a greater height. Rudimentary as it may be, the ability to play two tones should carry with it an effort at artistic accomplishment. I realize now, that to get this artistic expression, especially in the earlier stages, some adequate motive must be presented to call it forth."

"Yes," said Harriet, "my love for Mother and the wish to please her some way affected my desire to play my piece as beautifully as I could. If my teacher here had asked me to learn the piece to play it at some ordinary recital, my motive, I am sure would have been not love, but something like fear. I should have practiced, of course, but only so as not to disgrace myself. What you say about 'adequate motive,' if I understand these words, is that you must have not only a love for what you do, but also a love for the occasion in honor of which you are doing your work."

"That's a very wise observation," replied her uncle; "when you study the history of art, you will find that most of the great things have been done for the glorification of some great occasion, have been inspired by some spiritual or human love."

The refreshments had kept the younger members of the family busy while this discussion was going on. All now felt the necessity for some fitting close to the whole affair. The music of the celebration had so brought back to Mrs. Brown's mind her early musical experiences, that she involuntarily suggested that the group sing together one stanza of "Should Auld Acquaintance Be Forgot." All joined in the beautiful melody, the sentiment of old acquaintance receiving a significance because of the new acquaintance with the old that the united effort of making music together had made possible; and because of a new acquaintance with themselves, through the appreciation of the beautiful — a peculiar ministration for which music seems, of all the arts, most effective.

When the song was over, Jack, whose clear treble voice had that crystalline beauty that just precedes its change to the lower octave of the man, looked into his mother's face and exclaimed, "I love music!"

LIBRARY OF PIANO COMPOSITIONS

Suggested by Prof. Clarence G. Hamilton, of Wellesley College.

MUSICIANS' LIBRARY, Published by Charles H. Ditson.
> French Piano Music, Vol. 2 (Modern Compositions).
> Modern Russian Piano Music, 2 Vols.
> Piano Lyrics and Shorter Compositions by E. Grieg.
> Selections from the Music Dramas of R. Wagner (Otto Singer).

PIANO CLASSICS, 3 Vols.   The Schirmer Library, published by G. Schirmer.
> Sonata Albums, Vols. 329, 340.
> Anthology of Piano Classics, Vol. 1263. •
> Scandinavian Music, Vols. 1104–1105.
> Slav Piano Music, Vols. 1109–1110.

Editions published by the Boston Music Co.
> American Composers, Vol. 42.
> Italian Composers, Vol. 327.

A SELECTED LIST OF RECORDS WITH EXPLANATORY COMMENT

Prepared by Mr. Louis Mohler, A.M.

MUSIC FOR YOUNGER CHILDREN

Lullaby   *Brahms*

This may be had for Voice or arranged for First and Second Violins and Harp.

The Bee	*Schubert*	*Violin, Maude Powell*
Minute Waltz	*Chopin*	*Violin, Maude Powell*
March of the Little Lead Soldiers	*Pierné*	*Orchestra*

The music justifies its title. It has a well-ordered rhythm that suggests mechanical movement, as the march of lead soldiers.

Children's Toy Symphony	*Haydn*

A composition by a great master. Haydn himself played the piano the first time the music was performed. We can hear the tones of a violin and a bass viol. All the other instruments heard are toys; such as the cuckoo, the quail, the rattle, and the triangle.

Children's Toy March	*Currie*

This music gives an impression of dolls marching, each playing some instrument.

Minuet in G	*Beethoven*	*Flute, Cello, Harp*

This minuet by its rhythm impels to a slow gliding walk. The ends of its sections are so accented that one desires to bow or curtsey.

Spring Song	*Mendelssohn*	
Rondino (On a theme by Beethoven)		*Violin, Fritz Kreisler*

The simple little theme returns again and again throughout the composition, as the name implies.

Serenade	*Titl*	*French Horn and Flute*
Largo—from New World Symphony	*Dvořák*	*Philharmonic Orchestra*

It is said the composer got his inspiration for this part of his symphony from reading Longfellow's "Hiawatha." The melody given out by the English Horn is like a lullaby. Read the part of the poem, "Hiawatha," which tells about the wigwam of Nokomis on the shore of the lake.

Sweet and Low	*Barnby*	
Mighty Lak' a Rose	*Nevin*	

MUSIC FOR OLDER CHILDREN

Souvenir	*Drdla*	*Violin, Music*

The word signifies a remembrance, something that we keep to remember a place or person.

Serenade	*Moszkowski*	*Violin, Zimbalist*

In the music the violin sings to us a song of night.

Andante Cantabile	*Tschaikowsky*	*Boston String*
Op. 4		*Quartette*

The first word, "Andante," means a slow gentle movement. "Cantabile" means that the melody moves along in clear singing style.

Träumerei	*Schumann*	*Boston String Quartette*

Schumann wrote a number of music compositions that suggest scenes of his childhood. This is one of the best known.

Hungarian Dances	*Brahms*	*Orchestra*
No. 5 and No. 6		
Grande Valse—from	*Glazownov*	*Chicago Symphony*
the ballet Ruses		*Orchestra*
of Love		

The music is a chain of waltz melodies. There is a story of a Prince who came from far to meet his Princess. She, to tease him, dressed her maid as a Princess while she represented the maid. The first waltz melody is that of the Prince. He dances with the false Princess to the second melody. The real Princess dances before the Prince to the third melody theme — and now the Prince and real Princess end the story to the first theme.

(As danced by the Russian Ballet dancers.)

Madrigale   *Simonetti*   *Chicago Symphony Orchestra*

This is a short selection in the form of a song.

Moment Musical   *Schubert*   *Chicago Symphony Orchestra*

Schubert wrote a number of pieces for the piano which he called "Moment Musical." This one is a lilting melody that stimulates our imaginations. It is a picture of movement, perhaps a dance of Nymphs.

Danse Macabre   *Saint-Saëns*   *Orchestra*

The title suggests something gruesome. The music expresses in tones a poem called "The Dance of Death," by Casalis. The skeletons come out of their graves at twelve. One tunes his fiddle and the rest dance. This continues till dawn.

Iroquois Love Call   *Bentley Ball*

A bit of American Indian music, well sung and accompanied by an oboe and two Indian drums.

Hiawatha's Depar-   *Bentley Ball*
    ture (Westward)

A song originally sung at the departure of a traveler from Sault Saint Marie to the trading post where Detroit now stands.

Tribal Prayer   *Omaha*   *Bentley Ball*

A very short song or prayer in which a needy man addresses the Great Spirit.

My Bark Canoe   *Ojibway*   *Bentley Ball*

A lover's song in his bark canoe.

These four short selections are included in one record.

Overture to the Opera
     William Tell   *Orchestra*   *Rossini*

The overture is in four parts; each has a title.

The Dawn

This suggests the waking of day and the rising of the light over mountains and lakes.

The Storm

Descriptive music that represents the approach of a storm; how it breaks over mountains and trees and then passes in the distance.

The Calm

A tonal picture, at midday over a quiet lake among the Alps.

Finale

Music, martial in feeling. It recalls to our minds that the story of William Tell has to do with strife in battle.

Thou Brilliant Bird   *David*   *Sung by Marie Barrientos*

The music is from an opera called "Pearl of Brazil." The singer, so the story goes, walks in a great forest; the song of a bird and its brilliant plumage attract her. She sings to the bird; then she imitates its song.

Lo, Here the Gentle Lark Bishop   *Sung by Melba*

The words of the song are those of Shakespeare. The music in some parts suggests the flight of a bird, or the beauty of its song.

Ave Maria   *Bach-Gounod*   *Sung by Melba,*
                                                Violin by Kubelik

This is a prayer to the Madonna.

Overture to Midsum-   Mendelssohn   *Orchestra*
  mer Night's Dream

The overture follows the principal incidents of the story
by Shakespeare. After four prolonged chords we are in
Fairyland. Picturesque parts follow this music: the
hunter's horn; love music; a mock pageant in which we
hear the donkeys bray; an allusion to Bottom; then the
horn of Theseus and the dreamy beauty of the fairy music.

Intermezzo   *Mendelssohn*   *Orchestra*

The music follows the story of "A Midsummer Night's
Dream," and is played between Acts Two and Three.
There is a first part which suggests the emotions of Her-
mione when she finds herself alone. The music then
changes to a lighter vein and we have the march of the
clowns.

Nocturne   *Mendelssohn*   *Orchestra*

Night, and all is quiet. The mood of night is suggested
by the instruments used in the orchestra. The melodious
song is sung by horns and bassoons. The accompanying
instruments are the clarinets, oboes, and violins.

Valse Brilliante Op. Chopin   *Piano, Josef Hofmann*
  34, No. 1

The introduction is a flourish of brilliant tones and a
waltz theme which is sentimental in mood. This is followed by a swirling movement which leads into a dazzling,
dancing happiness.

Hunting Song   *Mendelssohn   Piano, Josef Hofmann*
Hark, Hark, the Lark Schubert-Liszt   Piano, Godowsky

Liszt used a melody that we often hear in a song,
but he adds many embellishments, rapid cadenzas
and trills.

He suggests to us the whirring flight of the lark, and the notes of its song.

La Campanella   *Paganini-Liszt*   *Piano, Godowsky*

The title means the song of bells. The first part, or introduction, was composed by the violinist, Paganini. The peal of bells is heard all through the music mingling with the principal theme.

Symphony in B   *Schubert*   *Orchestra*
Minor (Unfinished)

Someone says that the music suggests the sea — its restlessness and quiet; its great distances and intimate nearness. No matter, it is music to enjoy without connecting it with any explanation.

The Marseillaise   *De L'Isle*   *Sung by Leon Rothier*

The stirring music of the French National Hymn is often heard, but to get its full significance it must be sung in a manner that will reveal all its fiery eloquence.

The Star-Spangled   *Key*   *Sung by John Mc-*
Banner   *Cormack and chorus.*
                                           Chas. Harrison and
                                                          chorus

The music of our National Hymn is sometimes thought to be unsuited to its purpose. There are, however, several records of this music that will convince us of the grandeur and stateliness of the words and music.

The Swan   *Saint-Saëns*   *Played by Pablo Casals*

This is a picture in music — the melody suggests the slow, quiet, graceful movement of the swan. The accompaniment suggests the undulating surface of the water over which she moves.

Serenade	*Schubert*	*First and Second Violin and Harp*

In an arrangement for these instruments the Serenade of Schubert seems to gain in interest.

Orientale	*César Cui*	*Violin, Zimbalist*

The Russian composer tells us about a caravan in the Orient. It is really a picture made by the tones of the violin.

Funeral March of a Marionette	*Saint-Saëns*	*Orchestra*

This is a story. The music tells us that the Marionette fell, and was broken; its companions then carry it away and we realize their grief and understand the various incidents of the journey. A pleasant burlesque in good music.

Andante—from The Fifth Symphony	*Beethoven*	*Philharmonic Symphony Orchestra*

A Symphony is a great music story usually in four parts. This is the slow movement from perhaps the most famous symphony ever written.

Intermezzo	*Wolf-Ferrari*	*Chicago Symphony Orchestra*

The word "Intermezzo" means a part coming between. This music comes between Acts Two and Three of an opera called "Jewels of the Madonna."

Chorus of Dervishes Ruins of Athens	*Beethoven*	*Violin, Heifetz*

The Dervishes are whirling dancers of the Orient. The music in the rhythmic pattern of its melody suggests their movement.

Triumphal Entrance of the Bojaren	*Halvorsen*	*Philharmonic Symphony Orchestra*

In the Orient, the Bojaren were the ruling men of the realm, or the king's chief counselors. Whenever they entered the king's city they were received with great acclaim. In the procession were dancers and jugglers. The music tells this much better than we can explain.

Prelude to the Opera Lohengrin	*Wagner*	*Chicago Symphony Orchestra, Boston Symphony Orchestra*

Like Sir Galahad, Lohengrin was a Knight of the Grail. Tennyson tells us how the Grail came into sight before Sir Galahad. Wagner in his music tells us a similar story.

Procession of the Knights of the Holy Grail, in Parsifal	*Wagner*	*Chicago Symphony Orchestra*

The Temple of the Grail was many times the scene of great splendor. Especially was this true of the scene when all the knights in procession came to the Grail service. The music pictures it to us.

MUSIC OF GREATER DIFFICULTY

En Bateau	*Claude Debussy*	*Orchestra*

With a varied tracery of outline in tones, a suggestion of delicate tonal color and rhythmic patterns, the music pictures a boat on a lake.

Finlandia	*Jean Sibelius*	*Orchestra*

This is a symphonic poem for an orchestra. The composer, a native of Finland, is said to record in tones the impressions of an exile who returns home after a long absence.

Scheherazade   *Rimsky-Korsakow*   *Orchestra*
(Shĕ-hā'-rà-zä'-dà)

Two numbers of the music of a symphonic suite, the music of which suggests one of the stories of the beautiful Princess in the " Arabian Nights."
I. Sindbad's Ship.
The first record is the music, "Sindbad's Ship" — or his voyage.
II. The Fête at Bagdad.
We are in the city of Bagdad — it is an Oriental city, and the music suits its title. There is a wild dance which makes us think of a Tarantella.

Étude in G flat Major   *Chopin*   *Piano, Paderewski*
Op. 25 No. 9

The word "Étude" means a music study.

Quartette in C Major   *Beethoven*   *Flonzaley String*
Fugue   *Quartette*

A fugue is interesting because we catch ourselves noting the theme as it is carried through by the different players.

The Carnival   *Robert Schumann*   *Orchestra*

Schumann composed this music for the piano. It consists of short pieces representing recollections of friends, places, and incidents. Seven of them are arranged for the orchestra. (1) The Préambule is like a general statement made in a dignified manner. (2) Valse Noble, a waltz in grand style, the memory of an august personage. (3) Coquette, music that by its dainty, light, changing rhythms justifies the word. (4) Reconnaissance, music which suggests by its theme and interwoven color, a calm quiet feeling of devotion. (5) Paganini, a rapid movement and gay mood, the remembrance of a great artist. (6) Valse, this is beautiful dance music. (7) Aveu, an avowal, the bit that we may call "exquisite."

Come, My Heart's Delight — from Opera Marriage of Figaro	*Mozart*	*Sung by Marcella Sembrich*
I am Titania — from the Opera Mignon	*Thomas*	*Sung by Tetrazzini*

In this opera, there is a play within the play, and in this the character Felina acts the part of a Fairy Queen. This is her song in the play.

Celeste Aïda — from the Opera Aïda	*Verdi*	*Sung by Caruso*

The hero of the story must away to the war. He has loved the beautiful Princess Aïda. He sings about her, calling her "Heavenly Aïda."

Nocturne in E Minor	*Chopin-Auer*	*Violin, Eddy Brown*

The Nocturnes of Chopin have no story back of them, they are just poetry in music.

Caprice Basque	*Sarasate*	*Violin, Eddy Brown*

A Caprice is a form of musical composition in which a theme is repeated in a variety of whimsical ways.

Le Rouet D'Omphale	*Saint-Saëns*	*Paris Conservatory Symphony Orchestra*

Hercules, to prove his love to a Lydian Queen, consented to serve as a slave. Dressed as a woman, he worked at the spinning wheel.   The music in a simple way gives the imitation of the spinning wheel.

| *Prelude to The Deluge* | *Saint-Saëns* | *Paris Conservatory Symphony Orchestra* |

After an introduction by the orchestra, the violin takes up its theme.   The music illustrates how the violin as a solo instrument is supported by an entire orchestra.

| *The Angelus* | *Jules Massenet* | *Orchestra* |

Massenet calls one of his groups of compositions, "Picturesque Scenes."   This music is one of them.

| *The Fête Bohème* | *Jules Massenet* | *Orchestra* |

This is a second picture in music, as given by Massenet.

| *Turkish March* | *Beethoven* | *Violin, Heifetz* |

Beethoven once wrote music for a pageant or masque. Many nationalities were represented in it, and each had its characteristic music.   This is the music for the Turks.

| *Onaway, Awake Beloved* | *Coleridge Taylor* | *Sung by Paul Althouse* |

The Song is from Longfellow's "Hiawatha" — from the scene of the wedding feast.

| *Ah, Moon of My Delight* | *Lehmann* | *Sung by Paul Althouse* |

This song is from a cycle called "In a Persian Garden." The words are from the Rubaiyat of Omar Khayyam.

| *I have Lost My Eurydice* | *Gluck* | *Sung by Homer* |

This song is from the opera "Orpheus and Eurydice." This is the lament of Orpheus at the beginning of the story.

Shadow Song   *Meyerbeer*   *Sung by Galli-Curci*

The song is from the opera "Dinorah." The heroine in a moonlight scene sings to her shadow.

The Bell Song   *Delibes*   *Sung by Marie Barrientos*

In the Hindoo story, "Lakmé," we have the song by the heroine. The music itself tells us why it is called the "Bell Song."

Spring   *Grieg*   *Chicago Symphony Orchestra*

This is a poem of spring. It is sung by the strings of the orchestra. It is not a gay spring of which it tells, but one of quiet beauty and delicate colors.

Roman Carnival — An Overture by Berlioz   *Orchestra*

The music of the record makes us a part of the scene in the carnival. The English horn sings the song of a young man; of a company of entertainers; the guitar first accompanies the soloist, then other members of his party join with him. The scene changes. Now we see a company of dancers in a wild leaping dance, the Salterello.

Rienzi Overture   *Wagner*   *Orchestra*

The music follows Bulwer-Lytton's novel, "Rienzi." The plebeians decide to overthrow the government of King Orsini and place a Papal notary, Rienzi, in his stead. The trumpets sound out the challenge of the plebeians; the stringed instruments voice a prayer; there is a part next that suggests assurance; the prayer returns and the music ends with a vigorous battle hymn.

American Fantasy   *Victor Herbert*   *Philharmonic Symphony Orchestra*

U

A Fantasy in music means a composition of no regular form. In this selection are several of our patriotic, or national songs; melodies arranged for a large orchestra.

POPULAR MUSIC

Music that is Easily Understood: from Many Concert Programs

Melody in F	*Rubinstein*	*Cello, Pablo Casals*
Largo	*Handel*	*Cello, Pablo Casals*
Barcarolle — from	*Offenbach*	*Sung by Alma Gluck*
Tales of Hoffmann		*and Louise Homer*

The music is intended for soprano and contralto voices. It is sung in a scene representing Venice and the gondola passing along the canals.

Barcarolle	*Offenbach*	*Cincinnati Symphony Orchestra*

The music from the opera "Tales of Hoffmann," without the voices. The arrangement gives us an idea of the swaying barcarolle rhythm, a rocking movement like that of a boat on quiet water.

Danube Waltzes	*Strauss*	*Cincinnati Symphony Orchestra*

These are a chain of waltz themes, beautiful in melody and flow of rhythm.

Hungarian Rhap-	*Liszt*	*Orchestra*
sody, No. 2		

Originally, this is a piano composition, but we like it as arranged for a large orchestra. It becomes a vivid portrayal of Hungarian Gypsy melodies; it pictures the different moods of these people, — their love, hate, daring, and defiance.

| *Prologue — from the* | *Leoncavallo* | *Sung by Ruffo or* |
| *Opera Pagliacci* | | *Stracciari* |

The singer comes before the curtain and tells the audience what the story of the opera is about. At the close he sings "Ring up the Curtain," and the play begins and he is part of it.

Room for the Facto-	*Rossini*	*Sung by Titta Ruffo*
tum — from the		
Opera Barber of		
Seville		

There is a barber in the story, a very clever witty fellow. He helps everyone, and he is in great demand. He sings about himself. "It's Figaro here, Figaro there, Figaro everywhere."

| *Marche Slav* | *Tschaikowsky* | *Orchestra* |

The march opens with the angry pounding of a drum — a call, a menace, a summons to battle. Then, over this single note, is heard the wailing minor chant of a primitive people. After stormy preparation the chant is again intoned with all possible orchestral sonority.

Mad Scene — from the	*Donizetti*	*Sung by Marie Barrientos*
Opera Lucia di		*or Galli-Curci*
Lammermoor		

| *Toreador's Song from* | *Bizet* | *Sung by Amato* |
| *the Opera Carmen* | | |

The Toreador, the bull fighter, is the hero of the opera, and he tells about the glory of conquest in the bull ring while his admirers applaud his song.

Mother Machree		*Sung by John McCormack*
Ave Maria	*Schubert-Wilhelmj*	*Violin, Heifetz*
		or Ysaye

The melody is the Ave Maria of Schubert which sings the prayer to the Madonna.

Overture 1812   *Tschaikowsky*   *Orchestra*

The overture suggests several incidents in the life of a people. Napoleon had pushed his campaign near Moscow. The episodes in the music are the nation at prayer; the challenge and preparation for battle; the battle and victory; the rejoicing as the conquered army retreats. The Russian National Air is introduced.

Ballet of Music from   *Gluck*   *Philadelphia Symphony*
the Opera Orpheus   *Orchestra*

This is the music that is played in the scene called Elysian Fields, or the "Realm of Blessed Spirits."

Peer Gynt Suite   *Grieg*   *Orchestra*

The four numbers were among those which Grieg composed as incidental music for the drama "Peer Gynt" by Ibsen. Each part has a title and each part is suited to an incident in the story.

Morning

The sun rises over the hills; the shadows are pushed aside, and the mist lifts from the sea.

Hall of the Mountain King

Peer, wandering in the forest among the mountains, comes to the castle of the Trolls. He abuses their hospitality and they dance around him; in mad fury they hurl him down the mountain side.

Ase's Death

Peer comes to his mother's cottage and finds her dying. The music consists of one motive repeated over and over.

Anitra's Dance

Peer visits foreign shores.   He is in the desert in the tent of an Arabian Chief.   The girl Anitra dances for him.

Solveig's Song   *Grieg*   *Sung by Galli-Curci or Lucy Gates*

Solveig, the heroine of Ibsen's story, "Peer Gynt," waits the return of Peer to his native country.   As she is at her wheel, spinning, she sings this song.

Rhapsody España   *Chabrier*   *Orchestra*

Music that is brilliant;   an impression of a journey through Spain.   There are two principal dance themes: the Spanish Dance, Jota, fiery and dashing, and the Malaguena, langorous and sentimental.

Ballet Egyptien   *Luigini*   *Orchestra*

The music is interesting because of its novel rhythms and peculiar mood.

Final Duet from the   Verdi
Opera Aïda

This music is the closing scene of the opera.   The hero and heroine of the story are sealed in an air-tight vault under the temple.   They sing their farewell to earth. The chorus in the temple service above them, and the orchestra, together fill in a background of tone around the voices of the singers in the foreground of the picture.

The Tower Duet —   *Verdi*
from the Opera Il
Trovatore

The hero of the story has been imprisoned in the tower; he must die in the morning. As he is a troubadour, he accompanies himself on the guitar. He sings, and the heroine of the story comes under the window. It is their farewell to each other. The chorus in a distant church chants a prayer.

Printed in the United States of America.

www.ingramcontent.com/pod-product-compliance
Lightning Source LLC
LaVergne TN
LVHW021713080426
835510LV00010B/976